The Book of Deuteronomy

The Book of Deuteronomy

An Exposition by
Charles R. Erdman

BAKER BOOK HOUSE
Grand Rapids, Michigan 49506

ISBN: 0-8010-3379-9

PHOTOLITHOPRINTED BY CUSHING - MALLOY, INC.
ANN ARBOR, MICHIGAN, UNITED STATES OF AMERICA

Thou Shalt Love The Lord Thy God

With All Thine Heart, And

With All Thy Soul,

And With All Thy Might

DEUTERONOMY 6:5

Introduction

THE short chapters of this Hebrew classic contain a masterpiece of oratory, a significant chapter of human history, a matchless code of morals, and a unique expression of true religion. As the fifth book of the Bible, Deuteronomy completes the so called Pentateuch, the "five books of Moses," or the "five books of the law." The name given to this book is taken from the Greek translation and is understood to mean a "repetition of the law," or, literally, a "second law," from the Greek *dueteros* and *nomos*. The book does review the legislation recorded in Exodus, Leviticus, and Numbers; however, it is no mere copy of these statutes. It rehearses and amends the law under particular circumstances, with a special purpose and in an unusual literary form.

The circumstances were these: Israel had been delivered from bondage in Egypt, and at the foot of Sinai had made a covenant with Jehovah. The people were to obey His law and He was to be their God and King. To them the land of Canaan was promised as a possession. Yet when the desert had been crossed they turned back from the border of the land in disobedience and unbelief. During thirty-eight years of sojourn in the wilderness the older generation had perished, and now, as a new nation, the Israelites had reached the plains of Moab and were about to enter the Land of Promise.

It was, therefore, necessary for Moses, the great legislator, to rehearse the law already enacted, to adapt it to a people entering upon a permanent home, and to plead with them to renew their covenant with God and to be loyal and obedient to Him. Indeed, the sum and substance of Deuteronomy seems to be an arresting appeal for *obedience to God.*

The literary form of the message is a series of addresses or orations, all delivered within the period of a few days. In the preceding books, God is represented as speaking to Moses and revealing His law; in Deuteronomy, Moses is represented as speaking to the people and delivering his solemn words of farewell.

The First Oration (Chs. 1–4) is introductory, and it embodies the message of the whole book. It presents the gracious dealing of God with Israel as supporting the plea for gratitude and obedience to Him. The history of the people is reviewed from the time of their departure from Sinai until they are encamped on the plains of Moab. The chief experience of the first year is related in vivid detail. Israel had been brought in safety through the "great and terrible wilderness" to the border of Canaan, but there at Kadesh their disobedience and unbelief resulted in defeat and disaster (Ch. 1). The next thirty-eight years are passed in silence and then the story of the journey is resumed. Under the guidance of God great victories are won over Sihon, king of Heshbon, and Og, king of Bashan, and the country east of the Jordan is in the possession of the triumphant tribes (Chs. 2, 3). In view of such defeat and triumph, Moses presents his eloquent plea for devotion and loyalty (Ch. 4).

Thus this first address presents the goodness of God as the *motive for obedience*.

Following a statement relative to three "cities of refuge" and after a formal introduction (Ch. 4:41–49) the *Second Oration* is recorded (Chs. 5–26). This forms the main portion of the book. It is a résumé and an exposition of the law delivered at Sinai. The first section (Chs. 5–11) begins with a recital of the Ten Commandments (Ch. 5), and embodies an extended exhortation based largely on the First Commandment. The theme may be found in the most famous verse of Deuteronomy, "Thou shalt love the Lord thy God with all thine heart, and with all thy soul, and with all thy might" (Ch. 6:5). This exhortation is enforced by reference to the deliverance from Egypt, the mercies of the wilderness journey, the experiences at Sinai, and the assurance of an entrance into the rich land of promise.

The section which follows (Chs. 22–26) records statutes relative to religion, to justice and to private and social life. The law thus expounded was to be enacted as the law of the land by being written upon stones to be erected on Mount Ebal (Ch. 27), and was sanctioned by the most solemn statement of rewards and penalties (Ch. 28). Thus the law of God is presented as the *guide in obedience*.

The Third Oration was delivered at the ratification of the covenant and was the final appeal for loyalty on the part of the people (Chs. 27, 30). The appeal is based on the past mercies of God and enforced by a warning in case of apostasy and a promise of restoration following repentance. The time has come for Israel to decide: The choice is between obedience and life, or disobedience and death. Moses pleads for a wise decision. He recalls all that the Lord did for His people "in the land of Egypt," the guidance granted during "forty years in the wilderness," and the recent victories east of the Jordan. If the Israelites will cleave to the Lord they can dwell securely in the good land they are about to possess. Thus the faithfulness of the Lord is the *encouragement to obedience.*

The last chapters of Deuteronomy deal with the closing days in the life of Moses. The great Lawgiver already had exhibited sublime obedience to the will of God. When sentenced to death because of a rash act of anger and forbidden to enter the Land of Promise he courageously had continued his task. He had led the people through a wilderness, had conquered the kingdoms east of the Jordan, and on the plains of Moab he had delivered this farewell address, summarizing all his legislation and pleading with the people to be loyal to their covenant with God. Now, without hesitation, he surrenders his office and work to Joshua, his successor, and delivers the book of the law to the priests and Levites (Ch. 31). He composes an immortal song of praise to God (Ch. 32). He pronounces his blessing upon the people (Ch. 33). In full vigor of mind and body, with unfaltering step, he ascends Mount Pisgah; he catches a glimpse of Canaan and then alone meets death in the mountain solitude and is buried by angels in an unknown grave. He has been faithful to the last and his fidelity is regarded as worthy to be compared with the faithfulness of Christ (Hebrews 3:2). Thus Moses was himself a true *example of obedience.*

C.R.E.

Contents

I

THE FIRST ORATION Deuteronomy 1 to 4

Preface [Ch. 1:1–5]. The opening sentences of Deuteronomy introduce the orator whose eloquent appeals form the main body of the book. They also state specifically the exact time and place when the messages were delivered, and even intimate that in the discourses the speaker would "declare" or review or expand the law which had been delivered at Sinai.

The *speaker* was Moses, the famous liberator, leader, statesman, lawgiver and prophet. He had begun life as a prince in the court of Egypt, a child of Hebrew parents, but reputed to be the grandson of the king. When forty years of age, with heroic self-sacrifice, he determined to abandon his royal position and to ally himself with his people Israel, a race of slaves. Because of an act of rash presumption he was compelled to flee from Egypt and spent forty years as a shepherd in the land of Midian. Answering a divine call, he returned to Egypt and was enabled to deliver the Hebrew people from their pitful bondage. He led them across the desert to the foot of Mt. Sinai. There he received a revelation of the law of God. On the basis of promised obedience to this law a covenant was made. The Lord was to be King and the Israelites were to be His people. He was to give them the land of Canaan promised their forefathers centuries before.

Resuming their journey, they reach the southern border of the land, but there, in fear and unbelief, they turn back to sojourn in the wilderness for forty years, until all the older generation had perished and a new nation was ready to undertake the conquest of the land. Moses led the people through the desert and enabled them to conquer the territory east of the Jordan. It was his last exploit. He was forbidden to enter the land and was warned of his approaching death. Therefore, as the people were encamped on the plains of Moab he delivers his farewell message of which the Book of Deuteronomy is the record, and in which he pleads with his people to obey the law of God and to be faithful to their covenant.

The *hearers* are described as "all Israel." This is to say, the message was addressed to Israel as a nation. Not all the multitudes could be within the sound of Moses' voice, yet all were included in his appeal, and these last words of the great leader were to be the permanent guide and inspiration for the twelve tribes as they took possession of the new land and entered upon their national career. These twelve tribes, numbering hundreds of thousands, are not to be regarded as a mere mob of liberated slaves. They had been organized into a disciplined army. They had learned the lessons of defeat for disobedience; they had more recently gained confidence by notable victories. However, they were in need of the warnings and encouragements which the Book of Deuteronomy contains.

The *time* of this farewell message is declared to be "in the fortieth year, in the eleventh month, on the first day of the month," that is, in the fortieth year after the exodus from Egypt. Thirty-eight years had elapsed since the law was given at Sinai. For the guidance of the new generation it was necessary that the law should be rehearsed and expounded and adapted to the conditions of residence in the land which soon was to be the national home of Israel. This exposition of the law with the accompanying exhortation to obedience was given in a series of orations. These messages, designed to meet the needs of ancient Israel at a time of particular crisis, have proved to be of priceless value for the guidance of the people of God in all ages.

The *place* where Moses addressed the people is stated as being "on this side Jordan," or "beyond Jordan." This phrase was ambiguous. Whether it meant east of the Jordan or west of the Jordan depended upon the standpoint of a speaker or writer. It needed some qualifying phrase. Thus here the words are added, "in the land of Moab" (v. 5). The Israelites had conquered the land of the Amorites and also the territory of Og, king of Basham, and now were encamped opposite Jericho on the east bank of the Jordan. In defining the scene where the addresses were delivered, the author mentions other localities: "On this side Jordan, in the wilderness, in the plain over against the Red Sea between Paran, and Tophel, and Laban, and Hazeroth, and Dizahab. (There are eleven days' journey from Horeb by the way of mount Sier unto Kadesh-barnea)." All these places lay along the route which Israel had taken in the journey from Mount Sinai until reaching the plains of Moab.

Their mention summons to mind the past experiences of the people as recorded in Exodus, Leviticus, and Numbers, and forms a link between these books and Deuteronomy. The name Horeb (or Sinai) recalls the giving of the law which, as stated, Moses began to "declare" or to "expound" in the statement that Kadesh was only "eleven days' journey from Horeb." Only eleven days after leaving Sinai the hosts of Israel might have begun the conquest of Canaan, but at Kadesh, in unbelief, they turned back to perish in the wilderness. Now forty years have elapsed and a new generation is standing at the threshold of the land. A journey of eleven days is contrasted with the wanderings of forty years. These words are as sad as familiar: "It might have been." If there is rebuke or regret in the mention of Kadesh, there is also encouragement and hope in the record of victories over Sihon and Og. As disobedience resulted in disaster, so triumphs would be certain to issue from obedience and faith. Thus this brief preface is a significant introduction of the law and to the appeals for loyalty to God and His covenant.

THE HISTORICAL REVIEW [Chs. 1:6 to 4:40]

The Call to Advance (Ch. 1:6–8). In his First Oration Moses passes in brief review certain experiences of the Israelites as they journeyed from Sinai to the plains of Moab. He first calls to mind the command in obedience to which the journey had been begun: "Ye have dwelt long enough in this mount: turn ye and take your journey. . . . Go in and possess the land which the Lord sware unto your fathers." There is no need to interpret the words as implying a rebuke. They are rather an encouragement, embodying a divine promise. The people had dwelt at the foot of Sinai "long enough." A year had elapsed since their deliverance from Egypt. The time had been sufficient to prepare for the journey and for the conquest of Canaan. At Sinai the people had received the Law. They had promised obedience to God, and thus made a covenant which marked the birth of the nation. They had been organized as a trained army of warriors; yet they also had been given a ritual and a sanctuary by which they became a nation of worshipers. An intrepid soldier, who was also an inspired prophet, had been confirmed as their commander. To guide them a pillar of cloud and of fire had been provided and silver trumpets had been appointed to call them to action. Thus all was in readiness for the march. Then came the command, "Turn ye, and take your journey, and go to the mount of the Amorites, and unto all the places nigh there unto, in the plain, in the hills, and in the vale, and in the south, and by the sea side, to the land of the Canaanites, and unto Lebanon, unto the great river, the river Euphrates." Such was the Land of Promise. Yet the possession was conditioned upon obedience and faith. For a second time Israel had reached the borders of the land. The orations of Deuteronomy were designed to give them courage to enter in and to enjoy the inheritance which "the Lord sware" unto their fathers.

"Ye have dwelt long enough in this mount" might come as a call to many followers of Christ, particularly to those who have recently entered upon His service. They have dwelt long enough at Sinai where they learned the demands of the law. They have been given a divine Leader. They have been granted the guidance of the Comforter and have heard the peals of the gospel trumpet. They have been numbered in the hosts of the redeemed, and have learned to worship in the name of Christ. Before them lies a better land, and the rich experiences of a Christian life. To them the call has come, "Turn ye, and take your journey." There need be no delay. They may "go in and possess the land." The conditions are familiar. Following the "captain" of their "salvation," they are to "trust and obey."

The Aides of Moses (Ch. 1:9–18). Moses further reminds his hearers that while he was their divinely appointed ruler and judge, certain chieftains had been chosen to aid him in his task. This had been done at the suggestion of his father-in-law, Jethro, who had seen that Moses was overburdened by the details and demands of his office. This proposal had met with the approval of the people. Therefore, Moses had taken the "chief" of the tribes, "wise men and known," and had made them rulers over the people, "captains over thousands, and captains over hundreds, and captains over fifties, and captains over tens," to be "officers" among the tribes. Thus it had been arranged that "they judged the people at all seasons: the hard causes they brought unto Moses, but every small matter they judged themselves" (see Ex. 18:13–26).

Furthermore, Moses recalled the charge which at that time he had delivered to the judges. In large measure it was a repetition of the wise words spoken by Jethro. It forms an admirable directory for magistrates and judges in all nations. They should "hear" every case with patience. They should "judge righteously," without partiality, without respect of persons, whether "small" or great. They should be fearless, since the judge acts for God and is responsible to Him. They should be humble, recognizing that some cases may be so difficult as to require reference to a higher magistrate. This appointment of aides for Moses relieved him of crushing burdens and assured the people that they would be wisely led and justly ruled. It was a further preparation for their journey.

It may be noted that the Early Christian Church adopted the same principle when it began its career. The apostles were so burdened by the details of administering the funds for the poor that deserving members were being neglected. Therefore, certain subordinate officers were elected to undertake this particular task, so that the apostles might be free to devote themselves to the spiritual needs of the church. It is wise for all modern churches to be organized according to the same plan. Pastors and preachers, so far as possible, should be relieved of financial problems and secular tasks, that they may give themselves more "continually to prayer and the ministry of the word" (Acts 6:1–6).

Unbelief and Defeat (Ch. 1:19–46). In the main portion of his First Oration, Moses recounts to the people the disaster which had been occasioned by disloyalty, and also the victories which had resulted from faith (Chs. 1 and 2). Upon these two grounds he bases his eloquent appeal for faithfulness to their covenant and for trust in God (Ch. 3).

The disaster had been tragic, indeed. Israel had departed from Horeb (or Sinai) and by divine guid-

ance and aid had passed through what Moses
called "that great and terrible wilderness" and had
reached Kadesh-barnea, on the southern border of
Canaan. During the journey the people had shown a
spirit of discontent and faithless despair, and on
reaching Kadesh this had broken out into open rebellion. The story as recorded in the Book of Numbers
(Chs. 13 and 14), and as here rehearsed by Moses, is
somewhat as follows:

It had been decided that spies should be sent
ahead of Israel to learn the character of the land and to
discover the military strength of the inhabitants. As
to the land, there was perfect agreement in the report
with which twelve spies returned. The land was flow-
ing with "milk and honey," and as a sample of its
fruitfulness spies exhibited a single cluster of grapes
so large as to be suspended on a pole between two men.
As to the difficulties in the way, the reports were con-
flicting. Ten of the messengers declared that the great
walls of the cities reached to the heavens, the country
was controlled by giants, and conquest would be
impossible. However, two of the spies, Joshua and
Caleb, agreed as to the richness of the land, but urged
the people to press forward, saying, "Let us go up at
once and possess it, for we are well able to overcome
it." Notwithstanding this more favorable report, the
people "would not go up but rebelled against the
commandment of the Lord." In their hopeless terror
they even accused God of cruelty in delivering them
from bondage only to have them destroyed by the
hand of the Amorites. Moses had pled with them,
recalling the wonders wrought in Egypt and the
fatherly care God had shown them in the wilderness.

"Dread not, neither be afraid," he had insisted. "The Lord your God which goeth before you, he shall fight for you." But all was in vain. They would neither trust nor obey. They "rebelled against the commandments of the Lord," and remained stubbornly and sullenly in their tents. Then God had pronounced His solemn sentence: All the men who had been delivered from Egypt must die in the desert; only Joshua and Caleb could enter Canaan, and the children who had been born in Egypt and those who would begin life during the long wanderings of Israel in the wilderness. Even Moses was to be no exception. Many years after this tragedy at Kadesh, Moses became so provoked by the perversity of the people that he disobeyed God and spoke ill-advisedly with his lips, and was condemned to die outside the Land of Promise. Only a new-born generation could enter the future inheritance.

When this sentence was heard the people had been smitten with horror and remorse. "We have sinned against the Lord," they cried; "we will go up and fight, according to all that the Lord our God commanded us." They had "sinned," but they had not repented. They felt dismayed at the disaster they had brought upon themselves, but there had been no real turning to the Lord. They had proceeded at once to disobey and to defy Him. "The Lord said, Go not up, neither fight; for I am not among you." But they "rebelled against the commandment of the Lord, and went presumptuously up into the hill. And the Amorites, which dwelt in that mountain, came out against" them and "chased" them and "destroyed them" in Seir, even unto Hormah. "And ye returned," Moses reminded them, "and wept before the Lord; but the

Lord would not hearken to your voice, nor give ear unto you" (v. 45).

It was too late. Their opportunity had been lost forever. These men might have fought and conquered and entered upon the promised possession; but "they could not enter in because of unbelief." It was not faith, but presumption to attempt the conquest after their sentence of death had been pronounced, and in direct opposition to the command of the Lord. Their rash assault did not show courage, but emphasized their unbelief and rebellion. It was this tragic mistake which Moses was to use, near the close of his First Oration, in urging faith and obedience on this new generation as they stood on the border of Canaan. Their fate has been employed as a warning to those who are about to enter upon a Christian experience and who may be tempted to fall back in discouragement and unbelief: "Let us therefore fear," writes the apostle, "lest a promise being left us of entering into his rest any of you should seem to come short of it" (Hebrews 4:1).

Faith and Victory (Chs. 2:1 to 3:11). To warn the people against unbelief and disobedience, Moses has related the disaster which befell them at Kadesh on the southern border of Canaan. Now, to encourage faith and confidence in God, he passes in silence the events of thirty years and recounts the recent triumph over Sihon, King of Heshbon, and Og, King of Bashan. It is a story of divine guidance and human obedience. A second attempt to enter Canaan from the south was not to be made. Rather, the Israelites were to go eastward around Mount Seir, and then northward up the Jordan valley, so as to begin the conquest of the land by the capture of Jericho. Their course would lead them through the territory of Edom and Moab and Ammon. Yet they were warned not to attempt the conquest of these lands. Passing along the borders, they were allowed to purchase provisions and food and water, but were to make a peaceful progress. However, when reaching the river Arnon, they were encouraged to cross into the hostile territory of Sihon. A courteous request had been made to be allowed a peaceful passage through his domain, but had been harshly refused. When he attempted to attack the invaders with all his armed forces, he had suffered a disastrous defeat and Israel had seized the land from the Arnon to Gilead.

Next to oppose the progress of Moses was Og, the king of Bashan. He seems to have been the last of a race of giants who had held the territory of Heshbon as well as Bashan. His huge stature was intimated from the fact that his bedstead (or sarcophagus), long after exhibited as a relic, was thirteen feet in length and six in breadth, of course far longer than its royal occupant. This huge monarch and all his forces had been utterly destroyed, and Israel had come into undisputed possession of all the country east of the Jordan "from the river of Arnon unto mount Hermon."

In recounting these triumphs Moses made clear his view of divine government. He wished his hearers to share his belief. He regarded God as the absolute Ruler of all nations. He had forbidden Israel to attack the Edomites on the ground that God had given "mount Seir unto Esau for a possession." Nor could they attempt the invasion of Moab or Ammon, because their land had been assigned "unto the children of Lot for a possession." Yet all the territory of Edom and Moab and Ammon once had been held by giants. They had been displaced by these nations, which now are regarded as divinely appointed and rightful owners of the land. However, when Og, King of Bashan, had come out to oppose the victorious Israelites, the Lord had said to Moses, "Fear him not: for I will deliver him and all his people into thy hand." Thus all national boundaries and the fate of all nations were regarded as under the control of God. His providences were full of mystery, yet He was certain to deliver and to protect those who trusted in Him and sought to do His will.

The Land of Promise (Ch. 3:12–29). The land in the Jordan valley which had been conquered was well watered and afforded abundant pasture. Certain of the tribes of Israel cast envious eyes upon it. These tribes were rich in cattle and desired this land as a permanent possession. West of the Jordan, Canaan was still unconquered. Moses, therefore, allotted this rich territory to Reuben and Gad and the half tribe of Manasseh, on the condition that they should leave their families and possessions in their new homes, but that all the men of these tribes should cross the river and aid their brethren in the conquest of the land. This they agreed to do. The fact that part of the country promised to Israel had been secured and was being enjoyed, gave new confidence to the people whom Moses was now addressing and in whom he was seeking to awake a spirit of obedience and faith. The land east of the Jordan was an earnest and an assurance that, whatever obstacles lay in their path, the people of God were certain to be victorious and certain to secure all the land promised to their fathers.

Moses now reminds the people of his own experience. The conquest of the territory east of the Jordan had given him an overwhelming desire to see the rest of the land. He recalled his petition: "O Lord God, thou hast begun to shew thy servant thy greatness, and thy mighty hand. . . . I pray thee, let me go over, and see the good land that is beyond Jordan, that goodly mountain, and Lebanon." This had been the desire and hope of his whole life, but his request was refused. He had "spoken ill-advisedly" with his lips. The fault was really that of the people, but the penalty must be inflicted. Moses was to climb Mount Pisgah and was to see the land but was not to be allowed to enter in. The conquest of the country east of the Jordan was an encouragement to faith, but the fate of Moses was a warning to the people and a pitiful rebuke of disobedience and unbelief.

The Plea for Obedience (Ch. 4:1–40). Moses has reviewed the history of Israel as a basis for a solemn exhortation. This appeal forms the climax and the main message of his First Oration. In view of the past mercies and the punishments of God, it was the obvious privilege and duty of the people to obey His laws. The plea was largely summarized in the opening verse, "Now therefore hearken, O Israel, unto the statutes and unto the judgments, which I teach you, for to do them, that ye may live, and go in and possess the land which the Lord God of your fathers giveth you" (v. 1).

The laws were not to be enlarged nor diminished by human hands. Israel was not expected to amend the commandments of God but to obey them (v. 2). The deadly peril of defying His commandments had been demonstrated by the experience at Baal-peor, when, as a result of partaking in idolatrous rites, twenty-four thousand people died of a plague (v. 3). By obedience to the divine statutes the people would become eminent among the nations, which would be heard to say, "Surely this great nation is a wise and understanding people" (v. 6). These divine statutes which gave Israel their superiority were to be kept and diligently taught to their descendants (vs. 7–9).

The law had been delivered at Sinai under terrifying conditions: "The mountain burned with fire unto the midst of heaven, with darkness, clouds, and thick darkness" when the Lord spake "out of the midst of the fire." The people saw "no similitude," no shape, no physical form. They "heard a voice"; that was all. The solemn inference was drawn: If God had revealed Himself by no figure or image when giving His commandments and making His covenant, He should be worshiped under no visible image or form. Therefore, Moses forbids idolatry of every kind. The people were not to make as an object of worship any "graven image, the semblance of any figure, the likeness of male or female, the likeness of any beast . . . the likeness of any winged fowl . . . the likeness of anything which creepeth on the ground . . . the likeness of any fish that is in the waters"; nor were they to worship "the sun, and the moon, and the stars"; these were creatures designed to give light as the servants of man; they were not to be paid the homage and the reverence due to the Creator alone (vs. 10–19).

God could brook no disobedience to His law. He had brought the Israelites out of Egypt, and He expected them to be loyal to Him. Even Moses, the great deliverer, when exasperated by the people, had incurred the divine displeasure and had been forbidden to enter the Promised Land. Any more serious fault on the part of the people, particularly any act of idolatry, was sure to be punished, for "God is a consuming fire, even a jealous God" (vs. 20–24).

To further enforce his warning against idolatry, Moses predicts the punishments which would be inflicted in case of its practice. The people would be driven from the land, scattered among the nations, "utterly destroyed," wholly given to the service of false and impotent gods. However, penitence would result in pardon. This penitence must be sincere. It must not be mere sorrow for their suffering, but a serious endeavor to turn to the Lord. They would surely find Him if they sought Him with all their heart and with all their soul. "(For the Lord thy God is a merciful God)" (vs. 25–31).

As to no other people, God had revealed Himself to Israel to be the one living and true God. He had dealt with them as with no other nation, bringing them out of the bondage of Egypt by mighty acts and giving them His law amid the thunders of Sinai. Not because of their merit, but because of His love for their fathers and patriarchs, He had chosen them and was now to drive out hostile tribes before them and to give them the land for an inheritance. They should know, then, and consider "that the Lord he is God in heaven above, and upon the earth beneath: there is none else"; and His goodness should bind them to obey him. Thus Moses concludes his solemn plea (vs. 39, 40).

A similar appeal comes to the followers of Christ. He has revealed Himself as the only Saviour. He has spoken to us by His Word and Spirit. He has wrought for us a great deliverance, and He offers us life in all its fullness; therefore, we should live no longer for ourselves but for Him who for our sakes died and rose again (II Cor. 5:15).

The Historical Supplement [Ch. 4:41–49]

The closing verses of the chapter mark the end of the First Oration and contain an introduction to the Second. They record the significant fact that after the close of this first address, Moses appointed three places on the east side of Jordan as *"cities of refuge."* To these, one who had killed another without so intending might flee for safety. This merciful provision was in accordance with a divine command (Num. 35:14). Moses had been pleading for obedience; he followed his plea by a personal example, the record of which forms a fitting appendix to his oration. It was in a matter of real importance. Six such cities of refuge had been promised, three to the east and three to the west of the Jordan. The latter were appointed by the successor of Moses after the conquest of Canaan but now that the land "on this side Jordan toward the sun rising" had been conquered, Moses makes no delay and follows out the divine command so far as was in his power, and designates Bezer, Ramoth in Gilead, and Golan, in the territories just assigned to Reuben,

Gad, and Manasseh. The full regulations regarding these cities are elsewhere recorded (Num. 35:9–24; Deut. 19:1–13; Josh. 20:1–9).

The last verses (44–49) belong properly to the chapter which follows. However, they are not a part of the oration which that chapter begins, but they express the title, the time, and the place of that great address. They intimate that this oration contains the law which Moses set before the children of Israel, and that it consists of "testimonies" or attestations of the divine will, "statutes" or expressions of moral obligation, and "judgments" securing human rights. This "law" was set forth in the time when "the children of Israel came forth out of Egypt," that is, while they still were on their way from the house of bondage to the Land of Promise. It was spoken "in the land of Sihon," the place of their first victories, "on this side Jordan," where they now were encamped ready to complete the conquest of Canaan. This conquest and their inheritance were conditioned, however, upon obedience to the law which Moses is about to review.

II

THE SECOND ORATION DEUTERONOMY 5 to 26

HORTATORY [Chs. 5 to 11]

THE Decalogue (Ch. 5). The Second Oration of Moses comprises the main substance of Deuteronomy. It consists of two parts. The first contains exhortations and warnings to be true to the divine covenant (Chs. 5–11). The second records the laws and statutes which the people were to observe in the land of their inheritance. As to this covenant, Moses declares: "The Lord made not this covenant with our fathers, but with us, even us, who are all of us here alive this day." He wishes to impress upon his hearers their personal responsibility. His words are to be interpreted as meaning that the covenant was made not only with their fathers but with Israel as a nation, and therefore was equally binding upon those whom he was addressing.

Moses, therefore, begins his oration by quoting the Ten Commandments, for these were the basis of the covenant and the embodiment of all the great principles expressed in the subordinate statutes and judgments he is about to review and expound. These Commandments are the summary of all the duties which God requires of men. They are not obsolete but are of abiding and universal obligation. They express the regulations which are essential to human life and society. Moses did not discover nor originate them; it is his honor to have published them in their immortal form. Actions are not wrong because prohibited by the Ten Commandments. They are forbidden in the Ten Commandments because they are wrong.

Christ did not annul nor amend nor alter the Commandments. He regarded them as perfect (Matt. 5:20), and He interpreted them as applying not only to outward acts but to the desires and intent of the heart. He freed them from traditional misconceptions by showing their spiritual character. He insisted that to transgress them would be not only an injury to men but a defiance of God.

The followers of Christ are not under obligation to keep the ceremonial laws of Moses, but they accept the standards of the moral laws as rules of life. They are "free from the law" as a ground of acceptance with God, they are not free to break the law He has ordained for man. They fulfill its requirements out of gratitude to Christ and by the power of His spirit.

In repeating the Ten Commandments, Moses does not in all cases use the words as originally recorded (Ex. 20), but He refers to this authoritative form (vs. 12, 15, 16) as familiar to speaker and hearers alike. He is not bound to verbal repetition in referring to the law as the basis for His exhortations and warnings.

The *Preface to the Commandments,* "I am the Lord thy God, which have brought thee out of the land of Egypt, out of the house of bondage," is an integral part and a supremely important part of the

Decalogue. It relates all moral obligation on the revealed will of God, and it states that the motive for obedience to His laws is gratitude for His redeeming love.

The *First Commandment,* "Thou shalt have no other gods before me," or "beside me," forbade the worship of false deities in addition to Jehovah. The Israelites were tempted not so much to substitute strange gods in His place, as to share with other gods the allegiance due to Him alone. Thus Christians are not so much inclined to give up faith in their Lord as to divide with other objects their supreme devotion to Him.

The *Second Commandment,* "Thou shalt not make unto me any graven image," has no reference to art, to painting or to sculpture, but prohibits the making of material objects for worship. The Lord is a "jealous God," that is, He is grieved when the honor due to Him is paid to images created by man, when, indeed, His glory "is given to another" (Is. 42:8). As faith in God is the basis of moral action, so idolatry results in immorality and its evil consequences fall upon future generations. The results of sin, not its guilt, are transmitted. The inheritance from virtue is quite as real and far greater for "those who love God and keep his commandments."

The *Third Commandment,* "Thou shalt not take the name of the Lord thy God in vain," rebukes profanity and perjury, and also forbids the irreverent use of anything whereby God makes Himself known. An offender cannot escape punishment, "For the Lord will not hold him guiltless that taketh his name in vain."

In the *Fourth Commandment,* the obligation to keep one day in seven as a sacred day of rest makes special mention of such freedom from labor for servants. This is enforced by recalling that the Israelites had been slaves in the land of Egypt.

The Sabbath law was not abrogated by Christ. He taught by precept and example that one day in seven was to be observed as a day of worship and rest, broken only by deeds of necessity and mercy. The Christian Church has transferred the observance from the seventh to the first day of the week, so that the "Lord's Day" might celebrate the resurrection of Christ. As such, it does not call to mind the creation (Ex. 20:11), nor the deliverance from Egypt (v. 15), but the "new creation" and the redemption wrought out by our Lord.

The *Fifth Commandment,* "Honor thy father and thy mother," enjoins upon children loving obedience and regard for their parents. It is designated by Paul as "the first commandment with promise," as it assures well-being and length of days to those by whom it is observed.

The *Sixth* and the *Seventh Commandments,* "Thou shalt not kill; neither shalt thou commit adultery," were interpreted by our Lord as applying to anger and to impure desire quite as well as to murder and to other sinful acts. He did not mean that an evil thought is as great an offense as a wicked deed, but that it is as truly a breach of the spirit and intent of the law.

The *Eighth Commandment,* "Thou shalt not steal," clearly implies the right of private property. The denial of this natural law has no sanction in

Scripture. Our Saviour taught the principle of Christian stewardship, namely, that all wealth is a sacred trust, for the right use of which everyone some day must render an account. The "community of goods" practiced for a time by the Early Church in Jerusalem was not Communism. This custom was local, occasional, temporary, and voluntary. Christians sold or retained property as they thought wise or as charity might suggest. Unfair wages, unjust taxes, unfaithful labor, dishonest gains, are among the many forms of theft which at present endanger the social order and which this commandment forbids.

The *Ninth Commandment,* "Neither shalt thou bear false witness against thy neighbor," applies specifically to testimony in courts of law, and to any untrue statement affecting the good name of a neighbor; but it also clearly prohibits all falsehood, untruth and deception as contrary to the revealed will of God.

The *Tenth Commandment,* which condemns covetousness, shows most impressively how far the Decalogue transcends all other legal codes. It regards not merely acts and deeds but also concerns intentions and thoughts. Thus this comprehensive commandment forbids all evil desire for that which one may not lawfully enjoy.

MOSES AS MEDIATOR [Ch. 5:22–33]

When Moses has rehearsed the Ten Words, which later had been graven on "two tables of stone," he reminds the people of their request that God should speak to them no more directly as He had done "out of the midst of the darkness" and "out of the midst of the fire," but that He should speak through Moses as their representative and mediator. The terrors of Sinai had done their work. The people had come to realize their own unworthiness and the infinite holiness of God. The request was granted. It was accompanied by a touching appeal, expressing the yearning of the divine heart for the obedience of the people: "O that there was such an heart in them, that they would fear me, and keep all my commandments always, that it might be well with them, and with their children for ever!" (v. 29). The "commandments" had been spoken *to* Moses in the hearing of the people (v. 22), the further "statutes" and "judgments" expressing the will of God were spoken *through* Moses as a mediator. These were in harmony with the commandments but subordinate to them and adapted to the conditions of the people in the land which God was about "to give them to possess it."

The petition of the people expressed the instinct of the human soul that sinful man needs someone to stand between him and a holy God. The full reply, given through Moses at this time, as more fully recorded (Ch. 18:18, 19), contains a definite promise that a Messiah was to come. The "one mediator between God and men, the man Christ Jesus" (I Tim. 2:5). Moses follows the recorded promise by an appeal for obedience: "Ye shall observe to do therefore as the Lord your God commanded you." Thus the apostle pleads for loyalty to Christ: "for if they escaped not who refused him that spake on earth, much more shall not we escape, if we turn away from him that speaketh from heaven."

The Great Commandment (Ch. 6). "Hear, O

Israel: the Lord our God is one Lord: and thou shalt love the Lord thy God with all thine heart, and with all thy soul, and with all thy might" (vs. 4, 5). It will be remembered that our Lord declared these words to contain "the first and great commandment" (Matt. 22:38; Mark 12:29, 30). They comprehend the "first table of the law"; they constitute a universal rule of life; they are the soul and substance of the Book of Deuteronomy. The Hebrews have ever regarded them as the essence of religion. They are known as the "Shema" (hear), from the first word of the formula. Since early days they have been the opening sentence in the public worship of the Jews and have been repeated by them twice daily.

As Moses pronounces these words they may be regarded as virtually the text of a sermon which forms the following section of this Second Oration. This section is a series of practical exhortations urging the people to be loyal to their God (Chs. 6 to 11).

As conforming to this "great commandment," the law of God was to be kept continually in the minds and hearts of his people. By it their private and domestic and public life should be ruled everywhere and at all times, as Moses declares: "And these words, which I command thee this day, shall be in thine heart: and thou shalt teach them diligently unto thy children, and shalt talk of them when thou sittest in thine house, and when thou walkest by the way, and when thou liest down, and when thou risest up. And thou shalt bind them for a sign upon thine hand, and they shall be as frontlets between thine eyes. And thou shalt write them upon the posts of thy house, and on thy gates" (vs. 6–9).

Certain of these phrases have been interpreted by the Jews as literal commands. Small boxes containing the "Shema," and other short extracts from the law, have been bound upon the forehead and attached to the arm to conform to the words "a sign upon thine hand" and "frontlets between thine eyes." Moses is insisting that nothing should be allowed to make the people neglect the law of God. The prosperity which awaited them in the new land must not incline them to forget the Lord who had brought them out of Egyptian slavery (vs. 10–12). They should fear the Lord their God, and serve "him only" (v. 13), as the words are otherwise translated and as they are cited by Christ in answer to the Tempter (Matt. 4:10). It should be noted that all three of the memorable answers made by Christ to the Tempter (Matt. 4:4, 7, 10) were quoted from the Book of Deuteronomy and from this very section which applies the principles of the commandments to the life of the people (Chs. 6:13, 16; 8:3).

The second of these replies is taken from the same chapter: "Thou shalt not tempt the Lord thy God" (v. 16; Matt. 4:7). To "tempt" God is to put Him to a test, or to make Him act in a certain way to prove His goodness and His power. Thus "in Massah," when needing water, the people had cried out in unbelief, "Is the Lord among us, or not?" (Ex. 17:7). So here, when dire punishment has been threatened in case of idolatry, the people were warned not to put God to the test, not to make Him show His sore displeasure against those who presumed to break His law (vs. 13–16).

Moses assures his hearers that if they would keep

the commandments of the Lord it would "be well" with them, they would "go in and possess the good land" and their enemies would be "cast out" before them (vs. 17–19).

Furthermore, these "testimonies" and "statutes" and "judgments" were to be taught to succeeding generations. They were to be explained as the gracious provision of the loving God who had redeemed His people from the state of "bondmen in Egypt," and "for their good" had given them these laws. They should obey Him in gratitude and love. Such obedience would be their "righteousness." As it proceeded from the heart, such "righteousness of the law" would be in perfect harmony with the unchanging principle of "justification by faith" (vs. 20–25 and Gen. 15:6; Rom. 1:17).

Practical Exhortations (Chs. 7–11). As chapter 6 was an exposition of the First Commandment, so the chapter which follows is an application of both the First and the Second. It is in substance a *warning against idolatry* (Ch. 7). The nations in possession of the land of Canaan were utterly corrupted by the foul practices attendant upon the worship of false gods. Their inevitable doom was merely hastened by the invasion of Israel. The people of God could not have survived if surrounded by such neighbors. Not only the national life but the very existence of true religion was at stake. Therefore there came the stern command: "Thou shalt smite them and utterly destroy them; thou shalt make no covenant with them, nor shew mercy unto them: neither shalt thou make marriages with them. . . . Ye shall destroy their altars, and break down their images, and cut down their groves, and burn their graven images with fire."

Israel could have no possible complicity with idol worship, but must be wholly dedicated to the service of God. "For the Lord thy God hath chosen thee to be a special people unto himself" (Ch. 7:1–6). Israel was to be the Lord's "peculiar treasure" (Ex. 19:5), His "jewels" (Mal. 3:17).

Absolute loyalty to God is urged on three grounds. First, the nature of God has been shown in His dealings with Israel. He is a God who is certain to be true to His covenant promises. He had chosen Israel as His "special people," not because of their greatness or merit, "but because the Lord loved you, and because he would keep the oath which he had sworn unto your fathers, hath the Lord brought you out with a mighty hand, and redeemed you out of the house of bondmen, from the hand of Pharaoh king of Egypt" (v. 8). Yet He was a "jealous" God and would punish those who were untrue to Him. His covenant was not irrespective of their conduct. Their blessed relations with Him could be dissolved by sin (Ch. 7:7–11).

As a second encouragement to obedience, Moses emphasizes the material benefits assured to those who were true to their covenant promise: "Thou shalt be blessed above all people." Even physical health is here related properly to morality and godliness. Moses elsewhere includes the choice of food and the care of the body as a part of his religious system (Ch. 7:12–15).

The third word of encouragement is found in the assurance of the presence and power of God, who will give to Israel victory over all enemies. What He did to Pharaoh and to the Egyptians, "so shall the Lord thy

God do unto all the people of whom thou art afraid."
Yet the condition must be loving trust and true devotion. There must be no desire for "the silver and
gold" which was upon the idols, and no thought of
"bringing into one's house" anything related to idol
worship. Sometimes those who are unwilling to disobey the explicit commands of God look longingly at
the gains and enjoyments of those who make no pretense of belonging to Him and no endeavor to do His
holy will (Ch. 7:16–26).

In continuing his oration, Moses again reminds
his hearers that the past experiences of Israel should
furnish a sufficient incentive for obedience to God.
The same appeal, in substance, has been made before;
now it is stated that the needs of the people during
their wilderness journey, and the divine provision for
them, had been designed to teach Israel the lessons of
humility and trust (Ch. 8).

As Moses declared: "And he humbled thee, and
suffered thee to hunger, and fed thee with manna,
which thou knowest not, neither did thy fathers know;
that he might make thee know that man doth not live
by bread only, but by every word that proceedeth out
of the mouth of the Lord doth man live" (v. 3).

These words were the first of the three quotations
from this section of Deuteronomy which our Lord
employed in His conflict with the Tempter (Matt. 4:4).
They are commonly interpreted as meaning that man
has higher needs than nourishment for the body, and
that spiritual food is more important than bread. This
is quite true but rather aside from the point. Both for
Israel in the wilderness and for Christ in the hour of
temptation the exact and pressing need was precisely

physical food. Our Saviour refused to turn stones into bread, and trusted His Father to sustain His life by any means he might deem wise. To Israel, when the ordinary means of subsistence failed, the miraculous gift of manna was granted.

Not only so, but other physical needs had been divinely supplied. As Moses adds: "Thy raiment waxed not old upon thee, neither did thy foot swell, these forty years." That was to say, garments and sandals had been provided for them during all their wilderness journey. Usually this had been by natural means, from their flocks and herds, and by traffic with desert tribes. Whether thus or by special providence, their necessities had been met, and they had learned to depend upon the grace of God (vs. 1–4).

Now all the circumstances were to be changed. The people were about to leave the desert to enter a land rich and fertile and abounding in natural resources by which their daily wants would be met in abundance (vs. 5–9).

Therefore they are warned not to forget the lessons of humble trust and dependence learned in the days of hardship and privation. Moses pleads with the people: "Beware that thou forget not the Lord thy God . . . when thou hast eaten and art full and hast built goodly houses . . . and when thy herds and thy flocks multiply, and thy silver and thy gold is multiplied . . . and thou say in thine heart, My power and the might of mine hand hath gotten me this wealth. But then thou shalt remember the Lord thy God: for it is he that giveth thee power to get wealth" (vs. 10–18).

These words are needed by the people of God in

all ages, for the perils of prosperity are ever more dangerous than the trials of poverty. Moses, therefore, concludes the warning by a solemn assurance that those who forget the Lord shall "surely perish" (vs. 19, 20).

Another similar temptation assails one who is prosperous. He is inclined to attribute his success to his superior virtue and righteousness. Moses warns his hearers against cherishing any such vain illusion (Ch. 9). He insists that God is to give Canaan to the Israelites, not because of their goodness, but because of the inhabitants of the land and in view of the gracious promises made to the patriarchs of old. "Not for thy righteousness, or for the uprightness of thine heart, dost thou go to possess their land; but for the wickedness of these nations the Lord thy God doth drive them out from before thee, and that he may perform the word which the Lord sware unto thy fathers, Abraham, Isaac, and Jacob" (vs. 1–5).

As to any imagined merit on the part of the Israelites, Moses declares that they have always provoked the Lord to wrath, and have shown themselves to be a rebellious people. To substantiate this charge he recalls the tragic incident at Horeb. As soon as they had been delivered from Egypt and had reached the Holy Mount, when Moses had ascended its summit to receive from God the two tables of stone on which were written the Commandments, the people, under the leadership of Aaron, had made a golden calf as an object of worship. At the sight of this abominable idolatry Moses had thrown down and shattered the tables of stone as a symbol of the broken covenant with God. He had ground the image to powder and scat-

tered it in the brook of which the people had to drink.
Only because of his intercession were the lives of
Aaron and of the guilty people spared (vs. 6–21).

Again and again, during the forty years which
followed, the people had shown a similar spirit of
rebellion and unbelief, as when they cried out against
the Lord at Taberah (Num. 11:3) or at Massah where
they had "tempted the Lord, saying, Is the Lord among
us or not?" (Ex. 17:7) or at Kibroth where the "people
that lusted" had been smitten "with a very great
plague" (Num. 11:33, 34), and most notably at Kadesh-
barnea, where in disobedience they had turned back
from the very border of the Promised Land. It is
evident that Moses was justified in his charge: "Ye
have been rebellious against the Lord from the day
that I knew you." Surely Israel had no merit on which
to claim the help of God in the conquest of the land.
The very life of the nation had been continued only
in view of the unselfish intercession of Moses: "I
prayed therefore unto the Lord, and said, O Lord God,
destroy not thy people, and thine inheritance, which
thou hast redeemed through thy greatness, which thou
hast brought forth out of Egypt with a mighty hand.
Remember thy servants, Abraham, Isaac, and Jacob:
look not unto the stubbornness of this people, nor to
their wickedness, nor to their sin" (vs. 22–29).

As a result of this intercession, two new tables of
stone had been inscribed with the Commandments
which had been given to Moses, and had been placed
in the sacred ark as a sign that the covenant
was renewed between God and His chosen people
(Ch. 10:1–5).

Furthermore, after years of delay, the journey

toward the Land of Promise had been resumed. When Aaron, the great priest, had been compelled to forfeit his life for his fault at Meribah (Num. 20:23–29 and 33:38), Eleazar his son had been appointed to carry on his work; and the tribe of Levi had been ordained for its sacred service, "to bear the ark of the covenant of the Lord, to stand before the Lord to minister unto him and to bless in his name."

The nation had been spared, provision for worship had been made, the journey toward Canaan had been resumed, not because of any merit on the part of the people but because of the mediation of their great leader. As Moses declares: "And I stayed in the mount, according to the first time, forty days and forty nights; and the Lord hearkened unto me at that time also, and the Lord would not destroy thee. And the Lord said unto me, Arise, take thy journey before the people, that they may go in and possess the land, which I sware unto their fathers to give unto them."

Therefore, since all that Israel enjoyed had been granted in grace, Moses insists that there should be, in return, love and obedience toward God. "And now, Israel, what doth the Lord thy God require of thee, but to fear the Lord thy God, to walk in all his ways, and to love him, and to serve the Lord thy God with all thy heart and with all thy soul, to keep the commandments of the Lord, and his statutes, which I command thee this day for thy good?" (vs. 12–13).

This demand is further enforced by an impressive reference to the greatness and grace of the Lord. As He cares for the fatherless and the widow, all who serve Him should love the stranger even as God loved His people while they "were strangers in the land of

Egypt" (vs. 14–19). All that He had done for Israel since the days when their "fathers went down into Egypt" should incline them to "fear" Him, to "serve" Him, to "cleave to him" and to swear by His name. Their fathers had gone into Egypt as a household of merely seventy souls; now the Lord had made them a great nation, "as the stars of the heaven for multitude" (vs. 20–22).

"Therefore," Moses continues, "thou shalt love the Lord thy God, and keep his charge, and his statutes, and his judgments, and his commandments, alway" (Ch. 11:1). Israel should remember all the "chastisement of the Lord," that is, all His acts of mercy and of punishment, in Egypt and during their long wilderness journey. Of this gracious discipline Moses now selects certain familiar instances. He mentions the "miracles" in Egypt, that is, the plagues inflicted to effect the deliverance of Israel and the overthrow of the hosts of Pharaoh, "how he made the water of the Red Sea to overflow them"; and the marvelous support of the people during forty years of wilderness wanderings, and the severe punishment of the rebels who followed Dathan and Abiram. In that rebellion Korah had a chief part; but he is not mentioned, possibly because his sedition concerned religious authority, and Moses here is referring rather to the civil life of the nation which this defection had threatened (vs. 1–7).

In view of all this loving discipline of the Lord, Moses repeats his exhortation: "Therefore shall ye keep all the commandments which I command you this day, that ye may be strong, and go in and possess the land, whither ye go to possess it" (v. 8).

The very character of this promised land furnished another motive for obedience to God and
dependence upon His grace. In striking contrast with
"the land of Egypt," Canaan was wholly dependent
upon the gift of rain, which God might grant or
withhold. The fertility of Egypt resulted wholly from
the annual overflow of the Nile and an elaborate
system of irrigation. In a "land of hills and valleys"
such a system would be impossible; its harvests and
its grass for cattle could be enjoyed only as the Lord
sent the early and "the latter rain." Therefore, Moses
gives the specific warning: "Take heed to yourselves,
that your heart be not deceived, and ye turn aside, and
serve other gods, and worship them; and then the
Lord's wrath be kindled against you, and he shut up
the heaven, and there be no rain, and that the land
yield not her fruit; and lest ye perish quickly from off
the good land which the Lord giveth you" (vs. 8–17).

Israel was to be so absolutely dependent upon the
favor of God that the injunctions previously given
(Ch. 6:6–9) are repeated, to the effect that the commandments of the Lord are to be kept in mind continually by His people, and are to be taught diligently
to their children. If Israel was obedient to the Lord,
He would drive out the nations before them; they
would possess the entire territory promised to them;
no man would be able to stand before them, and
the dread of them would be "upon all the land"
(vs. 18–25).

This long series of exhortations closes impressively with a statement of the solemn sanctions which
were to be formally pronounced at a public ceremony
as Israel entered upon the new land—the blessing if

they obeyed, the curse if they were disobedient. The blessing was to be spoken on Mount Gerizim, the curse on Mount Ebal (see Ch. 27:12, 13). Such was the choice before Israel. Moses, however, is confident as to the future and sounds the note of assurance: "Ye shall pass over Jordan to go in to possess the land which the Lord your God giveth you, and ye shall possess it, and dwell therein" (vs. 26–32).

LEGISLATIVE [Chs. 12 to 26]

Laws Concerning Religion (Chs. 12:1 to 16:17). Here begins the second half of this oration. It illustrates the main purpose of Deuteronomy, which was so to repeat and amend the laws previously given as to adapt them to the conditions of the people who are entering upon their residence in Canaan. The first half of the oration has shown their relation to God who brought them out of Egypt (Chs. 5–11); the following chapters set forth the laws of the Land of Promise, (1) as the seat of divine worship, (2) as the sphere of divine government, and (3) as the home of God's people (Chs. 12–26).

First of all is the command to "utterly destroy all the places wherein the nations which ye shall possess served their gods," and the direction to provide for the nation one central place of worship (Ch. 12).

The provision of one such national sanctuary was an obvious necessity. Only thus could be secured the unity of the people and the purity of divine worship. If every Israelite had been allowed to select any place or any form of religious service he might choose, it is easy to see how great would have been the peril of lapsing into idolatry.

It was provided that animals might be killed for food in other places, but sacrifices could not be offered except at the national shrine. In no case, however, could blood be eaten; for "the blood is the life" and it belongeth to God (vs. 16, 23). All tithes, and firstlings and freewill offerings must be presented in the place which God might choose. While this prophetic provision of a national sanctuary was not fully realized until the days of David, and in the glory of Solomon's temple, yet God previously had appointed other places of worship, and there sacrifices were offered on special occasions and with divine sanction. Indeed, an "hour" was to come when, in the name of Christ, God was to be worshiped in no other place and under no other form, but "in spirit and in truth," as the Father of all who put their trust in Him (John 4:23).

The chapter closes with a solemn warning against being "snared" by the very idolators whose land they were to possess, and of being led to partake in the abominable rites of their pagan worship.

Among the sources of temptation to idolatry by which the Israelites might be "ensnared," Moses mentions three: a false prophet (Ch. 13:1–5), a near relative or friend (vs. 6–11), an apostate city (vs. 12–18). In every case those guilty of attempting such seduction were to be punished by death.

As to a prophet who sought to lead the Lord's people to worship "other gods," his words must not be heeded even though his message should be sanctioned by miracles. His invitation to idolatry would be a demonstration of depravity which no "sign" would or could refute.

As to temptation by a relative or friend, not even

the most sacred ties of natural affection must be allowed to draw away from loyal allegiance to the Lord who had shown His love as a Deliverer and Saviour.

Even when an entire city had been led away into apostasy by the influence of wicked and worthless men, the inhabitants were to be killed, the city was to be destroyed, the spoil was to be burned, nothing was to be kept by the avengers, and the city never was to be rebuilt.

These penalties may seem harsh, even cruel, but one needs to consider the different "manner of spirit" which characterizes the Gospel age, and most important of all, one must remember that Israel was a theocracy. God was the acknowledged King. To seduce one from absolute devotion to Him was an act of high treason, to be punished as such. Nor should the followers of Christ fail to note the parallel principles which are involved in their relationship to Him, and the influences today which tempt them to renounce their supreme loyalty to their Saviour and Lord. Even now false prophets are occupying places of wide religious influence and seem able to deceive even the elect. Holy relationships are urged by those who would draw Christian believers into lives of worldly, even sinful, indifference, and are giving new poignancy to the word of the Master: "He that loveth father or mother more than me is not worthy of me" (Matt. 10:37). Then, too, the force of numbers is hard to resist; when a city is "wholly given to idolatry" it is difficult to stand alone and to testify for the one living and true God and to plead with men to seek for salvation by faith and allegiance to His Son.

Having warned the people against temptations to idol worship (Ch. 13), Moses now prohibits practices and customs common among idolators (Ch. 14:1–21). For example, he forbids cutting the body or shaving the head as signs of inordinate grief or mourning. Such acts were performed by the heathen to propitiate false gods. These indignities would be quite unworthy of a people who were the "children of the Lord," the "first born" among the nations, whom the Lord had chosen to be His own special possession (vs. 1, 2).

On the same grounds care must be exercised by the Israelites in the choice of their daily food. They could eat no "abominable thing," that is, nothing which God hath forbidden. The distinction between "clean" and "unclean" had been more fully set forth in previous legislation (Lev. 11). Here Moses repeats the regulations in practically the same words. The changes are due to the new situation. The people are about to leave the wilderness and to dwell in a land of plenty where certain forms of food would be more abundant and others less likely to be eaten.

In both lists only those "beasts" could be eaten which had cloven hoofs and also "chewed the cud," and only those fish which had both "fins and scales." Fowls were "clean," except those specified, which, in general, were birds of prey. Reptiles were declared to be unfit for food.

No animal which had "died of itself," from which, therefore, the blood had not been drawn, was regarded as clean. "Strangers," that is, persons who were not Israelites, might be allowed to eat such flesh if they desired; it might also be sold to "an alien" who was bound by no such scruples as Moses set forth.

Evidently the distinctions between "clean" and "unclean" were designed to guard the nation against idolatrous practices and superstitions, as, for example, the peculiar prohibition, mentioned last of all, "Thou shalt not seethe a kid in his mother's milk" (v. 21). However, besides all the religious grounds which required the Israelites to make their choice of food in view of divine regulations and as the chosen and separate people of God, there must have been practical reasons which regarded the preservation of health and the avoidance of disease. The regulations announced by Moses have received the continued approval of all civilized nations. They embody a principle employed by the followers of Christ, namely, that the human body is sacred as the temple of the Holy Spirit, and "whether we eat or drink and whatsoever we do," we should "do all to the glory of God" (vs. 3–21).

Instead of following any heathen practice in the choice of food, the Israelites are bidden by Moses to show their special relationship to God by holy meals eaten at the sanctuary, where at the same time the worshipers would recognize a sympathetic relationship to their fellow men by caring for the needy. These meals were provided by tithes from the produce of the soil. Every third year the entire tithe was devoted to such charity. Thus care would be taken for the "Levite," who possessed no land, and for "the stranger and the fatherless and the widow." By this it would be indicated that the Israelites, while separated from all idolatrous peoples, formed one great nation of worshipers dedicated to the service of God.

In the same way the Holy Supper, the Christian sacrament, the most sacred of all feasts, represents not only a vital relationship to a divine Lord, but also the unity of all believers, one body united in a common faith and sharing a common life.

The regulation for the relief of the poor by providing a triennial tithe (Ch. 14:22–29), is followed by other provisions of a similar character (Ch. 15). The "Sabbatical Year" is here regarded as a *Year of Release*. According to previous legislation, this "seventh year" brought rest to the land and freedom for slaves, but here it also assures release from debts. This applied to Israelites, not to foreigners, and the purpose was that there should be among them no persons in actual want. The translation, "save when there shall be no poor among you," is rather confusing (v. 4). The reading of the margin is more accurate: "to the end that there be no poor among you." The law was not adequate to secure absolute equality and universal wealth; but if those who possessed worldly goods would share with the less favored, and particularly would be considerate in the matter of debts, the blessing of the Lord would so rest upon all the people that none would need to suffer actual distress. Such gifts of charity were to be made generously and without grudging. There always would be some men overtaken by poverty. "The poor shall not cease out of the land." Therefore the prosperous should "open their hands wide" to give relief, and should feel no regret in their hearts either for giving or for being called upon to give (vs. 1–11).

In the second place, the "Year of Release" should be celebrated by the emancipation of slaves. All Hebrews, whether men or women, who had fallen into servitude because of their poverty, were to be set free in the "seventh year." Furthermore, it mercifully was enacted that they should not "go away empty," but should be "furnished liberally," so that they would not be in a state of poverty, but would have the means to start life afresh. Such generous treatment of slaves is encouraged by the reminder that all the Israelites had once been bondmen in the land of Egypt and had been redeemed by the grace of their God.

The humane treatment of Hebrew slaves is further emphasized by the fact that some chose to remain in a state of voluntary and permanent servitude rather than accept freedom. In such cases the compact was sealed by a peculiar ceremony. The ear of the slave was pierced by driving an awl through it into a doorpost of the house which was to signify that the servants henceforth belonged to the household and would be obedient to the master's word (vs. 12–18).

In the third place, further provision was made for the poor in connection with the dedication to God of all the firstlings of the herds and the flocks. These firstlings were to be "sanctified unto the Lord," that is, regarded as belonging to Him, and not to be used by the owners for any ordinary uses: "Thou shalt do no work with the firstlings of the bullock, nor shear the firstlings of thy sheep." All without blemish were to be sacrificed and eaten at a sacred feast. At such feasts "the stranger, and fatherless, and the widow" were to "come" and to "eat and be satisfied" (Ch. 14:29). The firstlings that had any blemish were not to be regarded as sacred, but could be eaten in the home of the owner, and could be shared freely with such persons as might be in need. However, the blood was not to be eaten but was to be regarded as sacred and was to be "poured out upon the ground" (vs. 19–23).

In rehearsing the laws relating to religion, Moses reaches a climax by mention of three chief Hebrew feasts, Passover, Pentecost and Tabernacles. There were others, and they were more fully treated in the earlier legislation (Ex. 12, Lev. 23, Num. 28, 29). Here (Deut. 16:1–17) four features of these feasts were emphasized: (1) They were to be celebrated, not in private homes, but at a central sanctuary; (2) all the male members of the twelve tribes were to "appear before the Lord" as participants in these festivals "three times in a year"; (3) the occasions were to "rejoice before the Lord"; (4) special provision was to be made for the poor, for "the fatherless and the widow," by freewill offerings made in proportion to the means of the giver.

Passover, with its associated Feast of Unleavened Bread, was observed in "the month of Abib," the first month of the sacred year. This feast commemorated the deliverance of the Israelites from their bondage in Egypt. The sacrifice of the paschal lamb was a prophetic symbol of the lamb of God who was to "take away the sins of the world." The counterpart of this feast is found in the Christian sacrament. It likewise points back to a redemption which has been accomplished, and forward to a greater salvation, as those who partake in this supper of our Lord do so "until he come," expecting His return, when their salvation will be complete.

The Feast of *Pentecost* ("fiftieth" day) observed seven weeks after Passover, and therefore called the Feast of Weeks, was known also as the "Feast of First

Fruits," for then two loaves, from the grain of the completed wheat harvest, were presented to the Lord. It was prophetic of that Christian Pentecost, when there was presented to the Lord the first great band of believers bound together by the Holy Spirit as one body, the Church of Christ.

Tabernacles was joyfully observed in the seventh month. It commemorated the wilderness days when all Israelites dwelt in "tabernacles" or booths, and expressed gratitude to God for bringing His people into the Land of Plenty. It marked the gathering in, not only of the grain, but of the vines and the fig trees, and was known as the "Feast of Ingathering." It corresponds to modern Thanksgiving Day, and voices praises to God for the completed harvest. Also, prophetically, as Pentecost may recall the "first fruits of redemption," so Tabernacles has been taken to foreshadow a time when all nations shall be gathered into the garner of God.

Laws Concerning Justice (Chs. 16:18 to 21:23). When Moses turns to instruct the people on the establishment of courts in various parts of the conquered land, he evidently begins a definite division of his oration. The relation between the paragraphs and their exact classification are not obvious, but, in general, Moses is making provision for the administration of civil law and the securing of justice for the people. *Judges are to be appointed* who will show no partiality, who will not be blinded by bribes, but will "judge the people with just judgment" (Ch. 16:18-20).

While chiefly concerned with civil cases, these judges were to see that idolatry was punished. Groves were not to be planted for the purpose of idolatrous practices, nor wooden images to be erected as objects of worship (vs. 21, 22).

Nor should breaches of the law of sacrifice go unpunished. If a man or woman were accused of actual idolatry, there should be a fair trial, and if "at the mouth of two witnesses" guilt was established, the penalty of death by stoning should be inflicted (Ch. 17:2–7).

If a case too difficult to be settled by local judges should be presented, it could be referred for decision to the supreme court located at the central sanctuary. This court was to be composed of the chief justice and certain priests. It was to be, not a tribunal to which an offender could appeal, but a *court of reference* to which judges of the lower courts might present cases for final decision. Such decisions could be rejected only on pain of death (vs. 8–13).

The provision for appointing judges is followed, not unnaturally, by directions for *the choice of a king*. With statesmanlike foresight Moses anticipated such a contingency. Israel was a "theocracy." God was the ruler. Moses was merely His representative. Moses realized that the people, under the influence of surrounding nations, might wish to establish a monarchy. This he neither advises nor forbids. If the desire was merely for a particular form of civil government, the preference might be innocent and the king might be merely a viceroy regarding God as his sovereign. However, as was the case in the choice of Saul, the first king of Israel, the desire might indicate a spirit of rebellion against God or a failure to recognize the beneficence of His rule, and it might partake of the nature of disloyalty or treason.

Therefore Moses, centuries in advance of the event, gives explicit directions as to the character and condition of a sovereign who might be chosen. In the words of Moses, he must be one "whom the Lord thy God shall choose." He could not be a foreigner, but "from among the brethren shalt thou set a king over thee." He must "not multiply horses to himself," which would indicate a desire for war and conquest. Nor must he "multiply wives to himself," as was the custom with Oriental monarchs, who thus revealed their self-indulgence and love of luxury; such a custom would expose one to the temptation of idolatry, as was the experience of Solomon. Neither should a king "greatly multiply to himself silver and gold," which probably would involve burdensome taxation of the people. The positive and supreme requirement was that the king should have written for him a copy of "the law," possibly this very book of Deuteronomy. He should "read therein all the days of his life, that he may learn to fear the Lord his God, to keep all the words of this law and these statutes to do them." His was to be a government, not of caprice or personal tyranny, but a rule of law. Such a law-abiding and law-enforcing king would regard himself as on an equality with his people but also as a representative of God. So he would "prolong his days in his kingdom, he and his children, in the midst of Israel" (vs. 14–20).

The appointment of a king was not to supersede or supplant the office of the priest or the prophet. All three, the prophet, the priest, and the king, held permanent places in the divine economy. Each had a specific sphere and function: the prophet spoke to the people; the king ruled for God over the people.

Therefore, when Moses has mentioned the contingency of choosing a king, he turns next to speak of *the priests*. As to their apointment and duties, the main features had been set forth in previous legislation. Here Moses emphasizes only the provision for their support. He reminds his hearers that no landed property has been allotted to the priests and Levites and that they cannot live by agriculture. Their sustenance must be found in sharing the sacrifices brought to be offered in worship of God. "The Lord is their inheritance." Here Moses specifies certain choice portions of the "ox or sheep" which should be given to the priests, and also, in mentioning the first fruits, he adds that "the first of the fleece of the sheep" is theirs. He further directs that any Levites who preferred to leave the local altars and minister at the central sanctuary shall receive an equal share of the support enjoyed by those whom they find worshiping there.

As to *the prophet,* Moses has a twofold direction. First, he warns against all who speak falsely in the name of the Lord, and, second, he promises continuance of the office, which was to reach its climax in Christ. As to false prophets, the Israelites were to tolerate none of those forms of idolatry used to communicate with the unseen world. They should abominate all "enchanters," "witches," "wizards," and "necromancers" who sought to consult with the dead. In a theocracy, the pretense of speaking for God, and using the message to lead people to worship idols, was high treason in its worst form, and was punishable by death. Witchcraft during the Christian centuries was of a different character; application of these ancient laws was just as unreasonable as it was cruel.

As to a true prophet, Moses is soon to end his great career, but he predicts that the Lord will raise up another prophet like to himself. The reference is to the whole order of prophets, who at crises in the life of the nation appeared to represent God, and in His name to speak to His people. This promise received its complete fulfillment when God finally spoke through His own Son. Such was the definite assertion of Peter concerning Christ: "For Moses truly said unto the fathers, A prophet shall the Lord your God raise up unto you of your brethren, like unto me" (Acts 3:22). Thus we find in Christ the final antitype of all these Hebrew mediators. He is the divinely appointed Prophet, Priest, and King, whose service is eternal.

Moses further provided for the maintenance of justice by appointing *cities of refuge*. These were places to which one who had caused death unintentionally, by accident, and without "malice aforethought," might flee. This instruction was a brief supplement to the laws already given (Num. 35:9–34). Finally, three such cities were designated on the east side of Jordan, and three on the west, in different parts of the country, so located that they would be easily accessible to all who might be in peril. The design was to prevent the shedding of innocent blood, which might occur in case an "avenger" should act with haste, before an investigation had been made. These sanctuaries were not open to actual murderers. Any such who fled thither would be delivered over for the administration of justice (Ch. 19:1–13).

Not only a man's life, but also his means of livelihood, were to be regarded as sacred. So Moses warns against removing the *landmarks* from inheritance of a neighbor and so of trespassing upon his property (v. 14).

These and all other offenses were to be established on the testimony, not of one, but of two or three witnesses. As to *false witnesses,* they should be brought before a supreme court, and a penalty inflicted proportionate to the injury their false testimony may have produced: "Life for life, eye for eye, tooth for tooth, hand for hand, foot for foot." This familiar *lex talionis* was not interpreted by the Hebrews literally, but figuratively. Their history does not contain examples of bodily mutilation due to legal sentence. The principle allowed other forms of satisfaction. It taught, however, that all persons were on an equality before the law and that "the penalty should fit the crime" (vs. 15–21).

Israel was about to conquer Canaan by force of arms. Therefore it was fitting that Moses should give to the people some instruction as to the *laws of warfare.* His directions were quite limited, but evidently were inspired by feelings of mercy, and were designed to prevent all wanton destruction of life and property. They did not concern all the features of war, but would prevent the ferocity and barbarous excesses practiced by the nations in the days of Moses.

He proposed consideration for the Israelites themselves when summoned to battle. They were to be assured that, as servants of the Lord, He would be with them and fight for them against their enemies (Ch. 20:1–4). A man who had built a home but not occupied it might have his service deferred for a year, as also could one who had planted a vineyard, or one who was engaged to be married. Furthermore, those who were "fearful and faint-hearted" were allowed to return home. Competent leaders were to be provided for the various divisions of the armies (vs. 5–9).

In the case of a siege, a peaceful surrender by the enemy would result in the safety of even their men of war, but hostile resistance would be penalized by the death of the warriors. Women and children were to be taken prisoner, and the spoil was to be eaten. These provisions were not to apply to certain specified nations of Canaan; because of their abominable practices they were to be exterminated. For the building of bulwarks, and as material to be used in a siege, no trees which bore fruit were to be cut down, for these were designed to aid in the support of life, and were not to be destroyed (vs. 10–20).

A further testimony to the sacredness of human life was given in the provision for expiation, in the case of an *undetected murder*. The city nearest to which the dead body was discovered must be regarded as in some degree responsible for the crime. The elders must take a young heifer and put it to death in a lonely place and in the presence of the priests. Then they must "wash their hands over the heifer," declaring their own innocence and asking the Lord to remove the guilt from His people. Thus the crime was regarded as a concern not only of an individual but of the community. If the murderer could not be discovered, then the heifer must be regarded as taking his place, and by such a symbolic expiatory rite the guilt of the land was removed (Ch. 21:1–9).

From among the captives taken in war an Israelite might select a woman to be his wife. However, there was to be no haste or cruelty. A month must elapse before the marriage. The woman must renounce her former relationship and mode of life. Afterward she could not be sold nor treated as a slave. The regulation was designed to allow no other form of union than that of lawful marriage (vs. 10–14).

Polygamy was permitted but not encouraged. Its unfailing peril of bitter jealousy was indicated, and it was illustrated by previous and subsequent history. Favoritism was restrained. The rights of a first-born son could not be set aside by mere preference or caprice. An inheritance was divided into a number of parts exceeding the number of children by one. This extra portion fell to the first-born son. It was the sacred "birthright" (vs. 15–17).

Children had duties as well as rights. The very existence of the family and the stability of society depended upon filial reverence and obedience. Therefore, a *"stubborn and rebellious son,"* "a glutton and a drunkard," might be denounced by his parents before the elders of the city, and be condemned to death. Such a penalty must seem extreme, but the procedure was at least a limitation upon the irresponsible power of life and death granted to a parent by the laws of Rome and other nations (vs. 18–21).

The people were to "put away evil" by executing an offender. However, if a criminal was hanged, the body was not to "remain all night upon the tree." Otherwise, the land would not be cleansed but further defiled: "For he that is hanged is accused of God" (vs. 22, 23). To this law Paul makes significant reference when setting forth the atoning work of Christ and the redemption secured by His death: "Christ hath redeemed us from the curse of the law, being made a curse for us: for it is written, Cursed is every one that hangeth on a tree" (Gal. 3:13).

Laws Concerning Domestic and Social Life (Chs. 22:1 to 26:19). In the closing paragraphs of this great oration, Moses includes certain injunctions which do not convey the compulsion of law but concern actions which should arise freely as expressions of sympathy and kindness. For example, explicit directions are given for the treatment of *lost property*. It was not to be hidden or secretly retained when found by another, but was to be carefully guarded until it could be returned to its rightful owner (Ch. 22:1–3).

So too when an animal belonging to a neighbor had fallen under its burden one should help his neighbor in lifting it up, even when the parties had been at enmity with each other (v. 4 and Ex. 23:4, 5). Distinction between the sexes had been divinely instituted; therefore dress or other articles identified with one should not be appropriated by the other. The confusion might result in immodesty or immorality (v. 5).

Sympathy and consideration should be shown also to the lower animals, and a due regard to the sacredness of maternal life; so if a bird's nest was found with "young ones or eggs," the mother should be allowed to go free (vs. 6, 7).

Still more important was the preservation of human life. If a "new house" was built, a "battlement" or railing must be put around the flat roof, which in the Orient was commonly used for sitting or sleeping.

Otherwise, there would be constant danger of fatal accidents (v. 8).

All confusion of seeds in a vineyard should be avoided (v. 9). An ox and an ass should not be yoked together. One was regarded as a clean animal, the other as an unclean animal; and the disparity in size and strength would involve cruelty (v. 10). Garments were not to be woven of diverse materials. The reason may have been sanitary or symbolic. The general principle was that of genuiness and of avoiding confusion where separation was regarded as the divine ideal (v. 11).

Fringes were to be worn on garments to distinguish the people of God, intimating that care for such details of life were regarded as significant (v. 12).

The preceding verses of the chapter have dealt mainly with rules of kindness; those which follow contain laws concerning chastity and the sacredness of marriage. In contrast with all other nations, these laws of the Hebrews were strict, and the punishment was severe.

The first case mentioned is that of a husband who accused his newly-married wife of having been impure. If she was declared innocent he was publicly chastised, was compelled to pay her father a fine of one hundred shekels, and was never allowed to divorce her. If found guilty the wife was condemned to death by stoning (vs. 13–21).

The same penalty was inflicted upon adulterers if the woman was married or engaged to another man. One who did violence to a woman must die. In case of seduction a fine of fifty shekels of silver must be paid to the woman's father, marriage was compulsory, and divorce was not permitted. Incest, which was allowed by other Oriental peoples, was absolutely forbidden. Social purity was regarded as the immutable law of God; it was the safeguard of national life (vs. 22–30).

From his discussion of the sanctity of family life Moses now turns to consider the purity of the *congregation of Israel* as a whole. From membership in this commonwealth certain classes of persons were to be excluded. First of all, persons who had been mutilated according to pagan customs would be associated with idolatry and could not be accepted as worshipers. Bodily deformity does not disqualify one as a servant of God, but those were days of symbols and shadows. The physical defect was a symbol of the moral and spiritual imperfection which make the true worship of God impossible (Ch. 23:1).

So, too, one born of an unholy union was excluded forever (v. 2). Nor could an Ammonite or Moabite "enter into the congregation of the Lord." These people had heartlessly opposed Israel on its journey toward Canaan; and Moab had hired Balaam to curse Israel, although God had turned his curse into a blessing. The welfare of these nations was not to be promoted; individuals from among them might be naturalized in Israel, but as tribes they were under a ban for having shown hostility when they might have been friends and allies (vs. 3–6).

On the other hand, the Edomite or the Egyptian was not to be abhorred. It is true that Edom had refused the Israelites a passage through its land and that the Egyptians had held Israel in cruel bondage. However, the Edomites had descended from Esau, the twin brother of Jacob (or "Israel"); and Egypt had shown hospitality to Joseph and his brethren, and for centuries had allowed to their families residence in the richest portion of the country, before the years of cruel oppression had begun; this past kindness was not to be forgotten. Descendants in the third generation of Edomites or Egyptians might become naturalized Israelites (vs. 7, 8).

Measures were to be taken for preserving the *purity of the camp* in the time of war. Every man must keep physically and ceremonially clean. No defilement was to be allowed, because the Lord was to accompany the armies and in His presence there should be nothing unclean or unholy (vs. 9–14).

Kindness was to be shown to the *fugitive slave*. He was not to be surrendered to his owner from whose cruelty he had fled, but must be allowed to dwell in whatever place in the land he might choose (vs. 15, 16).

Prostitution was a common part of religious practice among idolatrous nations; but among Israelites this was to be regarded with abhorrence, and the gains of no such man ("the price of a dog") or of a woman could be presented in the "house of the Lord" in fulfillment of a vow (vs. 17, 18).

Usury was forbidden. At least, so the text reads. However, the prohibition probably applies to placing a cruel burden on a "brother," and to taking advantage of "the poor" (Ex. 22:25; Lev. 25:35, 36). It was declared to be proper to exact usury from a "stranger." If a loan to a merchant enabled him to make a profit, a portion of such gain properly belonged to the one who had made the loan. The words of Moses should not be interpreted to mean that investments are sinful or that the receipt of interest is immoral. In the parable of the "talents" (Matt. 25:26) our Lord rebuked the servant as "wicked and slothful" for failing to loan his money to the "exchangers" and for not returning his talent "with usury" (vs. 19, 20).

As covetousness might incline one to burden a poor brother by demanding a high rate of interest upon a loan, so it might tempt one to delay the payment of a vow, even when the promise had been made to the Lord. Moses insists that a vow is voluntary. It need not be taken, but when made the promise must be kept (vs. 21–23). As a further check upon selfishness, Moses enacted that in passing the vineyard or field of a neighbor one might take enough fruit or grain to satisfy hunger, but could carry away no store of such property (vs. 24, 25). The disciples of our Lord were criticized, not for plucking wheat as they passed through the fields, but for so doing on the Sabbath day. They were regarded as reaping grain and so of breaking the law of Sabbath rest.

The provisions made by Moses for *divorce* were interpreted by our Lord as due to the "hardness" of the human heart (Matt. 19:8). Divorce was not in accord with the ideal standard of the Law. At creation the divine intention was that the bond of marriage should never be broken. Divorce was a concession to the weakness of the Israelites. They had been infected by the loose practices of surrounding peoples who disregarded the sanctity of marriage. The Mosaic standards were as strict as could be enforced. Divorce was not encouraged. Its abuses were regulated.

Mention is made of one statute which was designed to prevent a rash or frivolous severance of the marriage tie. A divorced woman who married a second time could not be reunited with her former husband, even in case the second husband divorced her or died. Such a law would discourage hasty action on the part of a man and any displeasing conduct on the part of a wife (Ch. 24:1–4).

A second statute, designed to strengthen the marriage bond, is added. The *newly married man* was exempt from military service until the expiration of a year, and meanwhile he could not be burdened by an appointment to any public service (v. 5).

According to another merciful provision for domestic happiness, neither the "nether or the upper millstone" could be taken as a pledge. These were needed in preparing daily food. To remove either was to make it impossible to provide the necessities of life (v. 6). *Man-stealing* was punishable by death (v. 7).

Laws relating to *leprosy,* which were important on sanitary as well as on ceremonial grounds, were not to be relaxed in favor of the rich or powerful. They had been enforced even in the case of Miriam the sister of Moses (vs. 8, 9).

In taking a pledge for the payment of a debt, courtesy and consideration must be shown. The creditor should not enter the house of the debtor to select or seize a pledge, but must allow the debtor to come out to meet him. The debtor might be so poor as to possess little besides his garments, in which case the pledge should be returned by evening (vs. 10–13).

A *hired servant,* whether an Israelite or a foreigner, was not to be oppressed. Wages must be paid promptly lest the poor man should feel his need and cry out to God for justice (vs. 14, 15).

Unlike the practice of many ancient peoples, children were not to be punished for the crimes of their fathers, nor the parents for those of the children. Every one was to be accountable only for his own sin (v. 16).

Great kindness and care must be shown to "the *stranger,* the *fatherless,* and the *widow.*" The garments of a widow were never to be taken as a pledge, and for the relief of all these needy ones the gleanings of the fields and orchards were to be regarded as sacred (vs. 17–22).

Corporal punishment was not to be inflicted without mercy. The number of "stripes" was to be in accordance with the seriousness of the crime. In no case should they exceed forty. Greater cruelty might make the offender seem "vile" or contemptible. His dignity as a man must be respected, even in the case of a criminal (Ch. 25:1–3). The precept, "Thou *shalt not muzzle the ox* when he treadeth out the corn," refers to the custom of threshing by driving oxen back and forth over the grain which was placed upon the "floor." It is not to be understood only literally but as a proverbial prohibition against depriving a servant of his support. It was so used by Paul to enforce the truth that "they which preach the gospel should live of the gospel" (v. 4 and I Cor. 9:14).

Levirate marriage was so called from the word "levir" which is the Latin for "brother-in-law." The custom required that a widow should marry the brother of her deceased husband in case the latter had been living on the same family estate and had died childless. The purpose was to prevent a family from becoming extinct. The eldest child of such a marriage was to take the name of the dead husband and inherit the estate. A brother-in-law could escape the obligation only by a public declaration and humiliation. He could be brought before the judges, spit upon, and his shoe be untied by the widow. The removal of the shoe indicated that the man relinquished all claim upon the widow or upon the property of his brother.

The beautiful story of Ruth seems to indicate that the term "brother" might be more widely used to include a "kinsman." The story further intimates that the "brother" should purchase the property in which the widow had an interest, and so be designated a "kinsman redeemer." No more perfect type could be given of the redeeming work of Christ, who was "near of kin," was rich enough to redeem, and was willing to pay the price (vs. 5–10 and Ruth 4).

The levirate law insured the preservation of families, so no cruelty could be allowed which might take away the hope of offspring. The use of *unjust weights and measures* was not to be permitted. Such a practice always involves special injustice and hardship to the poor, and it destroys the foundation of all honest trade (vs. 13–16).

Kindness and sympathy, however, must not produce indifference to cruelty and crime. Thus, for example, the Amalekites must be punished. Heartlessly they had fallen upon the sick and faint Israelites who were struggling along in the rear of the hosts which had escaped from Egypt and were marching into the wilderness. A detachment under the leadership of Joshua had turned to defeat these treacherous foes; but later, when the Israelites were prepared, the

Amalekites were to be utterly destroyed. "The wages of sin is death" (vs. 17–19).

As his oration draws to a close, Moses prescribes *two liturgical forms* which were to be followed by the Israelites after they had been settled in the Land of Promise. Both were related to the social and domestic life of the people concerning which Moses had been speaking. The first was to be used as each of the worshipers presented to the Lord, in the central sanctuary, a basket of *first fruits*. The gift was to acknowledge that all Israel was and had, should be attributed to the goodness and grace of God. The presentation was to be accompanied by the following words, which were to be addressed to the priest: "I profess this day unto the Lord thy God, that I am come unto the country which the Lord sware unto our fathers for to give us" (Ch. 26:3). When the offering had been made the Israelite was to repeat the following thanksgiving: "A Syrian ready to perish was my father; and he went down into Egypt, and sojourned there with a few, and became there a nation, great, mighty, and populous: and the Egyptians evil entreated us, and afflicted us, and laid upon us hard bondage: and we cried unto the Lord God of our fathers, the Lord heard our voice, and looked on our affliction, and our labour, and our oppression: and the Lord brought us forth out of Egypt with a mighty hand, and with an outstretched arm, and with great terribleness, and with signs, and with wonders; and he hath brought us unto this place, and hath given us this land, even a land that floweth with milk and honey. And now, behold, I have brought the first-fruits of the land, which thou, O Lord, hast given me" (vs. 5–10).

The second formula was to be used when presenting the *special tithes,* which, on the third and sixth years, were given to "the Levite, the stranger, the fatherless, and the widow." The gifts were to be accompanied by the following declaration and prayer: "I have brought away the hallowed things out of mine house: . . . I have not transgressed thy commandments, neither have I forgotten them: . . . I have hearkened unto the voice of the Lord my God, and have done according to all that thou has commanded me. Look down from thy holy habitation, from heaven, and bless thy people Israel, and the land which thou hast given us, as thou swarest unto our fathers, a land that floweth with milk and honey" (vs. 12–15).

This second and longest of his discourses Moses concludes with a solemn exhortation. He has repeated the divine commandments in the hearing of the people; he now pleads with them to obey "these statutes and judgments" with the "whole heart and soul." He enforces his appeal by reminding them that they had plighted their troth to God "to walk in his ways"; and, in giving them His laws, God practically had confirmed His promise that Israel should be His "peculiar," that is, His "treasured people," and that if they kept His commandments, He would exalt them "above all nations." His purpose was that they might be an object of "praise and renown and glory," and, above all, be a "holy people" separated unto the service of God, that through them salvation might come to all the world (vs. 16–19).

III

THE THIRD ORATION DEUTERONOMY 27 to 30

THE LAW PUBLISHED [Ch. 27]

MOSES has rehearsed the law and has applied it to the condition of the people who were about to settle in the Land of Promise. He now turns to speak of the publishing of the law and the sanctions by which it was to be enforced. When the Jordan had been crossed the people were to erect on Mount Ebal "great stones, and to plaster them with plaster." This coating of lime on cement was designed to furnish a smooth surface on which were then to be written "all the words of this law." The essence of the Law was contained in the "Ten Commandments." All other statutes were applications of its principles. Just how many of these enactments were to be transcribed it is needless to conjecture. The action was symbolic. It was an acknowledgment that the law of God was to be the rule of life in the land which had been given to Israel as a possession.

Near these stones an altar was to be erected. On it were to be offered "burnt offerings," to indicate that the people were wholly dedicated to the Lord, and also "peace offerings," to show that those who kept the law of God could enjoy fellowship with Him (Ch. 27:1–10).

There also was to follow an impressive ceremony designed to set forth the blessedness of obedience to the Law, and, more definitely, the peril of any who might disobey. On Mount Gerizim were to be stationed six tribes which had descended from the two wives of Jacob, namely from Leah and Rachel; these six were to attest the blessings. On Mount Ebal were placed the remaining six tribes; they were to assent to the curses. Possibly in order that there might be two groups of six tribes each, Reuben was omitted from the first group, as this tribe sprang from a disinherited ancestor; and in the second Zebulun was included, the descendants of the youngest son of Leah.

In the valley between the two mountains the Levitical priests were to be placed. They were to announce the blessings and the curses to which the tribes were to "answer and say, Amen." It was thus that all the tribes were publicly to accept the Law and to recognize its solemn sanctions (vs. 11–13).

As preparatory to the promises and warnings recorded in the following chapter, the Levites were to pronounce twelve woes. These were to rest upon any who were guilty of idolatry, of disloyalty to parents or neighbors, or of unnatural crimes or acts of violence. To these imprecations the people were to say, "Amen" (vs. 14–26).

THE SANCTIONS OF THE LAW [Ch. 28]

The sanctions of the Law are set forth more fully as Moses continues his address. These paragraphs form one of the longest and most appalling chapters in the Bible. They begin, however, with a summary of the *blessings of obedience.* If Israel would keep His commandments the Lord would exalt the people above all the nations of the earth. This condition of loyalty to His law is repeated three times (vs. 3–13). The result would be blessings in all the relations of life, fruitfulness in labor, prosperity in all undertakings, victory over enemies, increase in wealth and in national dignity and power (vs. 1–13).

The *curses upon disobedience* which follow form a terrifying picture. They are placed in striking contrast to the blessings which have been proclaimed. They again cover all the relations and experiences of life. The people would be tormented by pestilence and disease. The ground would be parched by drought. The land would be invaded and ravaged. The bodies of those slain in battle would be food for the beasts and birds of prey. The foe would consume the fruit and produce of the land. Cities and fortresses would be so besieged that the desperate inhabitants would devour the flesh of their children.

One enemy in particular is specified as driving the people to such extremities of madness: "The Lord shall bring a nation against thee from far, from the end of the earth, as swift as the eagle flieth; a nation whose tongue thou shalt not understand: a nation of fierce countenance, which shall not regard the person of the old, nor shew favour to the young. . . . He shall besiege thee in all thy gates throughout all thy land, which the Lord thy God hath given thee" (vs. 49, 50, 52). The reference is probably to the Chaldeans, but it applies to other enemies of Israel, and finds its horrible fulfillment in the atrocities committed by the Romans at the destruction of Jerusalem.

Yet dispersion from the Land of Promise was not to end the calamities of Israel. Torn from the land of their fathers, scattered among the nations of the earth, this people was to "find no ease . . . but a trembling heart, and failing of eyes, and sorrow of mind." They would fall into captivity, would be sold for bondmen and bondwomen, and many of them would be regarded as too worthless to be bought even as slaves. These prophecies of the dispersion and distress of the Jews are among the most significant in Scripture; the fulfillment has been literal and complete. It must be remembered that the story is not ended. Some day Israel is to accept the "Deliverer," who "shall turn away ungodliness from Jacob," and "so all Israel shall be saved." The solemn warnings which fell from the lips of Moses were not heeded; however, they were a proper sequel to his long orations, which set forth most fully the contents of the Law. They proclaim the peril of those who would "not observe to do all the words of this law that are written in this book" (v. 58).

It must be noted that this ominous chapter does not end the Book of Deuteronomy. The covenant with Israel was renewed after Moses had uttered these arresting warnings, and bade the people farewell with words of blessing on his lips.

The Covenant To Be Renewed [Ch. 29:1–13]

The *covenant made with Israel at Sinai* was based upon the law revealed to Moses and by him announced to the people. On their part they engaged to keep the law, and on His part the Lord promised to be their God and to accept the people as His own "special possession," to bring them into a rich land and to bestow upon them His continual blessing. Some forty years have passed. Israel is now on the plains of Moab, and about to enter the Promised Land. Moses has rehearsed the law in a series of addresses. He is concluding his orations by a solemn appeal to the people to *renew the covenant* and to be faithful to its obligations.

The covenant was not to be new, except in the sense that it was to be accepted by a new generation and in a new situation. The appeal to fidelity is introduced by reminding the people of the past goodness and grace of God. He had wrought "great miracles" for them in the land of Egypt, although to the present day Israel had not appreciated His power and His love. For forty years He had sustained them in the wilderness, providing clothing and food. When they reached the borders of Canaan He gave them victory over Sihon the king of Heshbon and Og the king of Bashan, so that they were able to divide the land east of the Jordan as an inheritance for the tribes of God and Manasseh. Therefore they are exhorted to "keep the words of the covenant" that they might prosper in all their ways. This covenant is to be accepted by and for all the nation, for young and old, for masters and servants, and for proselytes from other lands. The purpose is that God may "establish" them to be "a people unto himself" and that He may be unto them a God, as He "had sworn" unto their "fathers, to Abraham, to Isaac, and to Jacob" (vs. 1–13).

THE FINAL WARNING AND APPEAL [Chs. 29:14 to 30:20]

Not for this generation alone was the covenant to be renewed, but for generations yet unborn. All are to be warned against the besetting sin of idolatry.

Israel has seen in Egypt, and among all the nations with which they have come into contact, the abominations which attended and resulted from the worship of images of "wood and stone, silver and gold." Anyone who, in defiance of the law and its solemn sanctions, shall "turn away from the Lord to serve the gods of these nations, . . . the Lord will not spare him," and "all the curses that are written in this book shall be upon him, and the Lord shall blot out his name from under heaven."

Such dire punishment will fall upon the whole land if the people are disloyal to God. The country will become like Sodom and Gomorrah; it will be "brimstone and salt and burning" in its pitiful desolation. When other nations shall say, "Wherefore hath the Lord done this unto this land," then men shall say, "Because they have forsaken the covenant of the Lord God of their fathers, . . . and the Lord rooted them out of their land in anger, and in wrath, and in great indignation, and cast them into another land, as it is this day" (vs. 14–29).

Against this dark background of desolation and gloom Moses sketches a picture of *possible restoration* and revival and a renewed enjoyment of the favor of God (Ch. 30:1–10). This, however, is conditioned upon a sincere and heartfelt repentance. If Israel shall turn from idols to the Lord with the whole heart and soul, then He will "turn their captivity" and gather the people "from all the nations" whither He had scattered them.

It is predicted that Israel will be restored to the covenant mercies of God only when they accept as their Messiah and Saviour Him who died, "not for that nation only," but also that He might "gather together in one the children of God that were scattered abroad," when there should be "one fold and one shepherd." This national conversion of Israel is prophesied by Paul (Rom. 11:26), who elsewhere indicates that such blessings will be realized not only by a converted "Israel according to the flesh," but also by a spiritual Israel whose "land of promise" is not limited to an earthly Canaan.

It may be noted that this passage is not a prophecy, but a conditional promise, embodying the principle that where there is true repentance God is always ready to pardon. It accords with the gracious invitation of Isaiah, "Let the wicked forsake his way, and the unrighteous man his thoughts: and let him return unto the Lord, and he will have mercy upon him; and to our God, for he will abundantly pardon" (Is. 55:7).

Moses insists that Israel cannot plead ignorance in case of disobedience to God and disloyalty to His covenant. His "commandment," His revealed will, is not "hidden" or "far off." It is not in some high heaven of mystery; it is not located beyond some distant sea. "The word is very nigh unto thee, in thy mouth, and in thy heart" (vs. 11–14). This is the very sentence which Paul quotes when urging Israel to accept the Gospel message: "The word is nigh thee, even in thy mouth, and in thy heart: that is the word of faith, which we preach; that if thou shalt confess with thy mouth the Lord Jesus, and shalt believe in thine heart that God hath raised him from the dead, thou shalt be saved" (Rom. 10:8, 9).

Thus, in proclaiming the Law, Moses has clearly set before Israel "life and good," that is, prosperity and salvation, and "death and evil," that is, doom and destruction. So he makes his final, solemn appeal: "Therefore choose life, that both thou and thy seed may live: that thou mayest love the Lord thy God, and that thou mayest obey his voice, and that thou mayest cleave unto him: for he is thy life, and the length of thy days: that thou mayest dwell in the land which the Lord sware unto thy fathers, to Abraham, to Isaac, and to Jacob, to give them" (vs. 11–20).

IV

THE LAST DAYS OF MOSES
DEUTERONOMY 31 to 34

THE RESIGNATION [Ch. 31]

IN view of his approaching death, and with the expectation that Israel was about to enter the land of Canaan, Moses had delivered the orations which form the substance of Deuteronomy (Chs. 1–30). In these addresses he had reviewed the Law and adapted it to the new conditions under which the people were to live.

Now to him the final call has come. His office must be surrendered to his divinely appointed successor, and the law must be entrusted to the priests. Moses was also instructed to compose a "song" which would be an abiding warning against unfaithfulness. This song is recorded in a following chapter (Ch. 32). To it is added a "blessing" pronounced upon the tribes by their departing leader (Ch. 33). The account of the death of Moses is recorded in the last chapter of the book (Ch. 34).

First of all, he speaks words of encouragement to the people and to Joshua (Ch. 31:1–8). He reminds the people that he has been forbidden to "go over this Jordan," but assures them that the Lord "will go over before them" and give them victory over the nations as He had given them the victory over the kings of the Amorites. He repeats the same assurance to Joshua, who is to serve in his place: "The Lord, he it is that doth go before thee; he will be with thee, he will not fail thee, neither forsake thee: fear not, neither be dismayed."

Moses then delivers a copy of the law to the priests, with the special instruction that it should be read to the people at the end of every seven years, on the occasion of the feast of Tabernacles. At this reading all were to be present, "men, and women, and children," and foreign sojourners as well. Such an observance would remind the people that the Law was the abiding rule of their lives and conduct. The time and nature of the particular festival, which was a period of national thanksgiving, might intimate to Israel that the Law of God was a precious gift designed to secure the prosperity and happiness of the people (vs. 9–13).

At the divine command, Moses and Joshua present themselves "in the tabernacle of the congregation." The Lord appears "in a pillar of a cloud" and delivers a charge to Joshua, assuring him of success in bringing "the children of Israel into the land" and repeating the promise, "I will be with thee" (vs. 14, 15, 23).

Just before delivering the charge, however, the Lord predicts the future apostasy of Israel and the consequent "evils and troubles" which would befall them, and directs Moses to compose the "song" which would be a "witness against the children of Israel." That is, it would attest the warning which had been given against apostasy; it would remind them of the great goodness of God toward the people who showed their unfaithfulness to be most base ingratitude, and, furthermore, it would indicate that, in spite of their failure and consequent suffering, the Lord would again have compassion on them and vindicate His character by His dealings with Israel and the nations (vs. 16–22).

Then Moses commanded the Levitical priests to take the book of the law and place it by the side of "the ark of the covenant." This was an appropriate place. The "tables of the law" were deposited inside the ark (Ex. 25:16; 40:20), so "the book of the law" was a comprehensive commentary on the commandments graven on the "tables of stone." This book was declared to be "a witness against" the people, in the same sense that the "song" of Moses was a "witness." It attested the grace and justice of God in His dealing with a nation which was certain to be rebellious and unfaithful after the death of Moses as it had been during the long years of his life (vs. 24–27).

Having composed his "song" of warning and "witness," Moses summons all the "elders" and "officers" to hear the message, as they were to be responsible for teaching the people the ode, which seems now to have been rehearsed "in the ears of all the congregation" (vs. 28–30).

THE SONG [Ch. 32]

The story of Israel's wilderness journey begins and ends with a song. The first was sung by the shore of the Red Sea; it was a song of triumph celebrating the deliverance from Egypt (Ex. 15:1–18). The second was composed on the banks of the Jordan; it sounded notes of warning as the people were about to enter the land of promise, and soon were to prove unfaithful to their God (vs. 1–43).

Both these songs, like the 90th Psalm, are ascribed to Moses. Their literary art, their lofty sentiment, their picturesque imagery, their beauty of expression, their depth of meaning, indicate that Moses was not only a wise legislator, an impressive orator, but also a poet of the highest order.

This second Song of Moses is in essence much like the substance of Deuteronomy, and has as its burden the themes which are familiar in Old Testament prophecies: the goodness of God to His people and their unfaithfulness to Him, His punishment of them by the hand of hostile nations, and their deliverance as these nations are destroyed.

In the introductory sentence (vs. 1–3), Moses calls upon heaven and earth to witness his message, which is of universal concern:

> "Give ear, O ye heavens, and I will speak;
> And hear, O earth, the words of my mouth."

He hopes that his instruction may fall on the hearts of all hearers with refreshing and fertilizing power, "as showers upon the grass," for he is about to praise "the name of the Lord," to whom all "greatness" should be ascribed.

The theme of the Song is stated in the verses which follow (vs. 4, 5). Here the strength and perfection of God are contrasted with the perverse and corrupt conduct of His people:

> "He is the Rock, his work is perfect;
> ....
> They are a perverse and crooked generation."

Their folly has been shown by requiting, with disloyalty and rebellion, Him who was their Father and
Deliverer (v. 6).

To emphasize their ingratitude, the people are
urged to "remember the days of old" and the unfailing goodness of God. When, in His providence, the
nations came into being, He had a special regard for
"the children of Israel" and reserved for them a land
proportioned to their needs. He had shown them such
kindness as one might show to a man lost in a horrible desert:

> "He led them about, he cared for them;
> He kept them as the apple of his eye."

His discipline of them had been like the care of an
eagle teaching its young to fly:

> "As an eagle stirreth up her nest, fluttereth over her young,
> Spreadeth abroad her wings, taketh them,
> Beareth them on her wings:
> So the Lord alone did lead them,
> And there was no strange god with him."

He alone had saved them; therefore they should serve
Him alone. To them He had given a land of honey
and oil and milk, rich in all the products of vineyards
and fields (vs. 7–14).

"But Jeshurun waxed fat, and kicked." The so-
called "Righteous Nation," like a pampered ox that
had become unmanageable, rebelled against the Lord.

> "Then he forsook God which made him,
> And lightly esteemed the Rock of his salvation.
> They provoked him to jealousy with strange gods,
> With abominations provoked them him to anger" (vs.
> 15, 16).

For this sinful apostasy God would severely punish His people. This determination is set forth in predictions of dire disasters.

"And when the Lord saw it, he abhorred them, . . .
And he said, I will hide my face from them,
I will see what their end shall be" (vs. 19, 20).

The fire of divine wrath will break forth. Famine and the sword, wild beasts and pestilence, will be the instruments by which the penalty will be inflicted. The people would be utterly destroyed were it not for the respect which God has for His own name. He would not allow the enemy to ascribe to their power the punishment which was the work of the Lord. The gods of the enemy were impotent:

"For their rock is not as our Rock,
Even our enemies themselves being judges" (v. 31).

The only explanation of Israel's defeat and distress was to be found in their disobedience and rebellion and consequent punishment (vs. 19–33).

The purpose of God, however, is the reformation and deliverance of His people and the destruction of their enemies. Such is His fixed purpose.

"Is not this land up in store with me,
And sealed up among my treasures?" (v. 34).

God would have compassion on His servants. He would show them the worthlessness of idols, and convince them that He alone is God. The Lord as an avenger is represented as a warrior, armed with sword and arrows:

"If I whet my glittering sword, . . .
I will render vengeance to mine enemies. . . .

I will make mine arrows drunk with blood,
And my sword shall devour flesh."

For this retribution upon His enemies the nations should praise the Lord; and the Song closes with this appeal:

"Rejoice, O ye nations, with his people:
 For he will avenge the blood of his servants,
 And will render vengeance to his adversaries,
 And will be merciful unto his land, and to his people"
       (vs. 34–43).

When Moses, with Joshua, has rehearsed this Song in the hearing of the people, he adds a solemn admonition to them to keep all the commandments of God, for this is no matter of indifference, but a condition of the very existence and prosperity of the nation:

"It is not a vain thing for you; because it is your life"
       (vs. 44–47).

On the same day that Moses taught the people this national ode, the command previously given (Num. 27:12–14) was repeated. He was to ascend Mount Nebo, and was to survey the Land of Promise, but was to die in solitude. The command had in it the pathos of a sentence pronounced because of disobedience and momentary disloyalty to God; it had in it at least a faint gleam of immortality, for the hero was to be "gathered to his fathers." This seems to mean more than the gift of a lonely grave, even if it lacks the assurance of those who know that, with their loved ones, they are to be "forever with the Lord" (vs. 48–52).

THE BLESSING [Ch. 33]

After the divine prediction of the death of Moses, and before the account of that event, there is recorded the blessing which Moses pronounced upon the tribes as his farewell message to Israel.

It is closely related to the Song which Moses had just rehearsed in the hearing of the people. Both anticipate the future; but they are strikingly contrasted. The Song is pervaded by dark clouds of coming failure and apostasy and punishment; the Blessing is bright with expectation of divine favor; there are no clouds and no shadows.

The Blessing finds a counterpart also in the farewell message delivered by Jacob to his twelve sons (Gen. 49). In neither case are there to be found clear and extended predictions of the future. There are rather interpretations of the various names and prophetic glimpses of the development of the tribes.

The benedictions are introduced by an adoring mention of the Lord who is the Creator and King of the nation and the Source of all its privileges (vs. 2–5). Then follow the blessings upon the several tribes (vs. 6–25). The conclusion is in praise of the Lord as the Refuge and Shield of His people (vs. 26–29).

The very origin of the people and the beginning of all their advantages are traced to the majestic appearance of God at Sinai. There He revealed a glory like the splendor of the rising sun. Through Moses, He gave His law as an abiding possession. In His love He accepted Israel as His people, and covenanted with them to accept Him as their King (vs. 2–5).

The order in which the blessings were pronounced does not correspond with the relative ages of the sons of Jacob or the position of the tribes in the camp, or their allotments in the Land of Promise. The principle of arrangement followed by Moses is difficult to determine. It seems, however, to be in accordance with the comparative character of the blessings as predicted and as realized in the developing history of the tribes.

Reuben, the eldest son of Jacob, is first to be mentioned. Because of grievous fault he had forfeited his birthright, yet his descendants were not to lose a place among the tribes:

> "Let Reuben live, and not die;
> And let not his men be few" (v. 6).

Simeon, the next in age, is passed in silence, possibly because, according to Jacob's prediction, his families were to be scattered abroad in Israel. As they were largely absorbed by Judah, they may be regarded as sharing in the blessing of this tribe.

Since *Judah* was to be the royal tribe and the champion of the people, the prayer for Judah may be a petition for a safe return from victorious campaigns (v. 7).

In the prayer for blessing upon *Levi,* the petition is that the Thummin and the Urim might abide with the godly Aaron, or with Moses as the representative of the tribe. These mysterious objects, worn in the breastplate of the high priest, were understood to be instruments for learning the divine will. The privilege so granted to the tribe of Levi is based on the loyalty of the tribe when tested at Massah and Meribah, when the people rebelled and when even Moses and Aaron stumbled. Also, because of the devotion of Levi to the Lord even at the sacrifice of the strongest natural ties (Ex. 32:26–29), Levi's tribe received the privilege of teaching the people and of presenting their sacrifices to the Lord. It was asked that their service might be acceptable to God and that they might be delivered from all their enemies (vs. 8–11).

Benjamin was the beloved son of Jacob, and his tribe is also beloved of the Lord and will dwell in safety, sheltered and protected by Him (v. 12).

The longest of all the benedictions is pronounced upon *Joseph,* the name used to designate the tribes which were descended from his two sons, Ephraim and Manasseh. The blessings are those of a fruitful land, favored with dew and rain, and with hillsides rich in olive trees and vines. This precious heritage will be due to Him who appeared to Moses in the burning bush and exalted Joseph when he "was separated from his brethren." These tribes will have power to thrust down hostile nations "even to the ends of the earth." These, thus blessed, "are the ten thousands of Ephraim, and the thousands of Manasseh" (vs. 13–17).

Zebulun and *Issachar* are to rejoice in their labor and in their rest. They will call nations to the mountain of the Lord and offer sacrifices acceptable to Him. Theirs shall be the treasures of both sea and land (vs. 18, 19).

The Lord is praised for His enlargement of *Gad.* This warlike tribe is likened to a lion in fierceness and strength. Gad chose for himself the first part of the conquered land, and is praised for faithfulness to his promise and for marching at the very head of the hosts for the conquest of the territory west of the Jordan. He obeyed God, fulfilling all His requirements, in company with the tribes of Israel (vs. 20, 21).

Dan is likewise compared to a young lion ready to spring from its lair in Bashan and to seize upon its prey (v. 22).

Naphtali is promised prosperity and divine favor. He was to possess "the west [literally 'the sea'] and the south." The territory did not border on the sea, but the tribe was to enjoy riches as of the sea, and also of the genial and fruitful south (v. 23).

Asher was to be blessed in surpassing measure. He would be favored by his brethren. His land would be rich in olive trees. His fortresses would be like iron or brass. His strength and security would last as long as his life:

"As thy days, so shall thy strength be" (vs. 24, 25).

This "Blessing" upon the tribes of Israel is concluded with an ascription of praise to the Lord from whom alone the promised benefits could come:

"There is none like unto the God of Jeshurun,
Who rideth upon the heaven in [for] thy help,
And in his excellency on the sky" (v. 26).

The God of Israel is called "the God of Jeshurun" (Chs. 22:15; 23:5, 26). This word probably means "the righteous one," and Israel had been called to be "the righteous one" among the nations.

For this people God was to be a Dwelling Place and a Protection:

"The eternal God is thy refuge,
And underneath are the everlasting arms."

Israel, victorious over all enemies, and separated from other nations, would "dwell in safety alone," secure in its own rich "land of corn and wine."

> "Happy art thou, O Israel:
> Who is like unto thee,
> O people saved by the Lord!" (vs. 26–29).

THE DEATH AND BURIAL [Ch. 34]

The story of Moses' death is one in which triumph and tragedy unite. It records the heroic close of a noble and significant career, yet it relates the punishment for a pitiful and pathetic failure. The event is narrated with notable restraint and in a few simple phrases.

When Moses has pronounced upon Israel his farewell benediction, then in uncomplaining obedience to God, and with unfaltering step, he climbs the slopes of Mount Nebo, there in solitude to meet the mystery of death. From this high summit he is granted a view of the Land of Promise. His clear vision sweeps from the mountains of Moab on the east to the Great Sea on the west, from the territory of Dan on the north, down the valley of the Jordan southward to the Sea of Salt.

It is not necessary to suppose that this sight was either a dream or a miracle. From the eminence on which he stood, the undimmed eye of the great leader could easily survey a wide prospect of Canaan. This impressive view was a gracious provision. The country he beheld was the one he had longed to see; it had been the goal of his endeavor through all the long years of his trials and his toil. There it lay before him, in all its glory. The sight was a great privilege, yet also was a tragic experience. It was the immediate prelude to the penalty of death. He heard the solemn sentence pronounced again: "I have caused thee to see it with thine eyes, but thou shalt not go over thither" (vs. 1–5).

Then the record continues: "So Moses the servant of the Lord died there in the land of Moab, according to the word of the Lord. And he buried him in a valley in the land of Moab." The method of the burial is useless to conjecture. That "God buried him" may mean no more than to describe a lonely resting place prepared by no human hands, as the history states: "No man knoweth of his sepulchre unto this day" (v. 6).

There is deep mystery about this death and burial. It is said that Michael the archangel contended with the devil and "disputed about the body of Moses" (Jude 9). When or where or why, is not known. Centuries after his burial, Moses appeared in bodily form, sharing with Christ the splendor of the "Mountain of Transfiguration" (Matt. 17:2, 3). In that scene there was present also Elijah, a man who had never died. Here are intimations of resurrection and immortality, of divine pardon, of future glory. Moses, at last, was in the Land of Canaan, but he had no desire to linger there. He had found "a better country, that is, an heavenly."

His earthly career had ended while he still was in full vigor of body and mind. "Moses was an hundred and twenty years old when he died; his eye was not dim, nor his natural force abated" (v. 7). No wonder that "the children of Israel wept for Moses in the plains of Moab thirty days" (v. 8). At the time when they were to attempt the conquest of Canaan, at a crisis when his guidance seemed to be most needed, their great leader was taken from them. To him they owed the creation, the organization, the preservation of their national life. They often had disobeyed him, betrayed him, disregarded him; now they recognized something of his greatness, his patience and his power, and realized their irreparable loss.

However, Joshua, the son of Nun, took up the task of leadership. As is often said: "God buries the workman but carries on the work." This new leader "was full of the spirit of wisdom; for Moses had laid his hands upon him, and he did as the Lord commanded Moses" (v. 9). As a wise and courageous commander, he secured for Israel the conquest of the land and apportioned it among the tribes.

Speaking in the language of types and symbols, it may be said to have been fitting that Moses should die outside the land of Canaan. Moses typified law, and only Joshua, whose name means "Jesus," could bring the people of God into the land of promised "rest," for "the law came by Moses, but grace and truth came by Jesus Christ."

However, as a matter of history, there is deep significance in the statements which close the narrative: "There arose not a prophet since in Israel like unto Moses whom the Lord knew face to face." He was a more colossal character than Joshua the fearless warrior who followed him. Moses was a distinguished soldier, and a wise lawgiver; but his pre-eminence lay in his close association and fellowship with God, by whom he was known "face to face."

As a result of such fellowship, he had been empowered to work "signs and wonders" in the land of Egypt for the deliverance of his people, and to perform mighty and terrible acts "in the sight of all Israel" (vs. 10–12).

No prophet "like unto Moses" did arise until He came whom Moses himself predicted in the word given him by the Lord: "I will raise them up a Prophet like unto thee, and will put my words in his mouth; and he shall speak unto them all that I shall command him" (Ch. 18:18). This prophet was none other than Jesus Christ our Lord, who, as Peter declared, has been sent to bless us (Acts. 3:22–26).

As we "hear him," and yield ourselves to his service, we learn the real lesson of Deuteronomy, namely, that *the experiences of life are disciplines* designed to teach us obedience and trust while we journey onward toward "the land of far distances" where we shall "behold the King in his beauty."